AT HOME IN MANHATTAN

AT HOME IN MANHATTAN Modern Decorative Arts, 1925 to the Depression Karen Davies

New Haven, Connecticut
Yale University Art Gallery
1983

This catalogue is made possible by a generous
grant from The Henry Luce Foundation, Inc.

A contribution from Susan Morse Hilles has provided
essential support for the exhibition.

Frontispiece (Figure 1.)
Eliel Saarinen, Dining Room,
"The Architect and the Industrial Arts,"
The Metropolitan Museum of Art, 1929.
Photograph courtesy The Metropolitan
Museum of Art.

Published in conjunction with an exhibition
held at the Yale University Art Gallery,
10 November 1983–5 February 1984

In 1973 the Mabel Brady Garvan Galleries opened at the Yale University Art Gallery, and for the first time at this institution, the American arts were presented as a continuum from the seventeenth to the twentieth centuries. The galleries reflected the strength of Yale's collections in the seventeenth and eighteenth centuries and the relative poverty of its holdings in the nineteenth and twentieth centuries. In fact, the furniture on display jumped in chronology from a 1905 tea table by the arts and crafts designer Gustav Stickley to the post-World War II chairs of Charles Eames. Building the collections in the period between the two world wars became an obvious curatorial priority.

Karen Davies, a graduate student in the Department of the History of Art, came to the American Arts Office in the fall of 1981 as a National Museum Act Fellow. She was assigned the task of cataloging a group of recent gifts of objects from the years 1930 to 1950. Some of these were given by Keith Smith, B.A. 1928, and others were donated by Jane Ritchie in memory of Andrew C. Ritchie, Director of the Gallery from 1957 to 1971. Upon completing the cataloging, Ms. Davies was asked to develop a list of decorative arts from the period between the two world wars suitable for acquisition by the Gallery. In the course of her research she became increasingly aware of the richness of this phase of American design and the dearth of information about its objects. In fact, American designs and designers of this period had largely fallen into oblivion. Sensing the need for an examination of the decorative arts from this era, Ms. Davies proposed to develop an exhibition proposal under the direction of Jules D. Prown, Professor of the History of Art, and myself. In the spring of 1982 her proposal was approved, and plans moved ahead for this exhibition and catalogue.

The research, planning, and organization of "At Home in Manhattan" could not have been carried forth without the support of the Friends of American Arts at Yale. Numerous colleagues and individuals have also freely given their time and assistance. Wilma Keyes and W. Scott Braznell were especially helpful in sharing their libraries and research files.

One of the important roles played by a university art museum, in addition to giving students access to works of art, is to provide practical museum experience. Kim Sichel, a National Museum Act Fellow in 1982–83, filled the critical post of exhibition coordinator and devoted countless hours to myriad administrative details. Gordon Sands, a Marcia Brady Tucker Fellow, provided invaluable assistance with the research. Deborah Federhen, a National Museum Act Intern in 1982–83, helped with proofreading the catalogue. Shannon Koenig, Marguerite French, and Marion Vaillant, all undergraduates, conscientiously assisted with numerous clerical tasks.

Many of the objects in the exhibition had not previously been photographed for publication, and the task of compiling illustrations for the catalogue was more formidable than usual. We wish to acknowledge E. Irving Blomstrann, Geri T. Mancini, Joseph Szaszfai, and Charles Uht for their extraordinary efforts in recording these images on film. Greer Allen, the University Printer, and John Gambell, Staff Designer at the Yale University Printing Service, gave constant guidance with the publication. The publication's crisp, clean design is testimony to the skills of its designer, Karen Salsgiver. We are grateful also to Robin Bledsoe, the editor, who gave the manuscript its final polish.

Certainly we owe a great debt to our fellow colleagues at the Gallery, without whose support this exhibition could not have taken place. Kathleen Giglietti, my secretary, and Diane Hoose, Business Manager, tended to many administrative details. David Barquist, Assistant Curator of American Decorative Arts, carefully read the manuscript, oversaw publicity, and consulted on the final installation. Daniel Rosenfeld, Acting Curator of Prints and Drawings, and Theresa Fairbanks, Paper Conservator, provided assistance with conservation problems. Rosalie Reed, Registrar, and her staff supervised the loans and transportation with their usual efficiency. Robert M. Soule, the Building Superintendent, and his staff meticulously carried out the exhibition design and installation. To all of these individuals we are deeply grateful. We are greatly indebted to Alan Shestack, the Henry J. Heinz II Director of the Gallery, for his constant moral support and endless energy in finding funding for this project.

We are particularly appreciative of the generosity of the lenders who have consented to part with their objects for the duration of the show: John Axelrod; Glen Bailey; Rosalie M. Berberian; Diana Diederich Blake; The Brooklyn Museum; The Chrysler Museum; Cooper-Hewitt Museum; Mr. and Mrs. William Hunt Diederich; Louise Rorimer Dushkin; Martin Eidelberg; Mimi Findlay; The George Walter Vincent Smith Art Museum; Ruth and Seymour Geringer; Nathan George Horwitt; International Silver Company; Muriel Karasik Gallery; Sydney and Frances Lewis; Suzanne Lipschutz; Richard A. Lukins; Peter P. Marino; The Metropolitan Museum of Art; Alan Moss Studios; Museum of Fine Arts, Springfield, Massachusetts; Albert Nesle; The Newark Museum; Philadelphia Museum of Art; Estate of Ruth Reeves; The Rockwell Museum; Mr. and Mrs. Lee M. Rohde; Suzanne Vanderwoude; Wadsworth Atheneum; George H. Waterman III; Wharton Esherick Museum; Diane Wolf; and many private collectors. We are also deeply grateful to The Henry Luce Foundation, Inc., for providing the funds to publish the catalogue. In particular we thank the foundation's officers, Martha Wallace and Robert Armstrong, for their invaluable assistance.

Karen Davies has chosen objects that delight the eye and offer an eloquent introduction to the decorative arts produced in America during the late 1920s and early 1930s. Her interpretation of these objects brings long-needed insights to this phase of modern design in America. Like many pioneering ventures, "At Home in Manhattan" may raise as many questions as it answers, but Ms. Davies has fulfilled her foremost goal—providing an assessment of a neglected period in the history of American design. From the time she first conceived of this project, she has dedicated herself to it with prodigious amounts of energy and a rare degree of intelligence. Working with her has been an uncommon pleasure.

PATRICIA E. KANE
Curator of American Decorative Arts

Numerous individuals generously shared time, expertise, and information with me in the course of organiz-ing "At Home in Manhattan." Alan Shestack provided essential support and encouragement from the exhibition's inception. Jules David Prown also served as an initial adviser and supporter and remained an insightful critic throughout every stage of the project's development. I am indebted to several members of the Yale University Art Gallery staff, including Richard S. Field, Kathleen Giglietti, Michael Komanecky, Mimi Neill, and Rosalie Reed. Barbara Heins, Robin Latham, Christine Poggi, Gordon Sands, and Rebecca Zurier contributed greatly to this project. Mr. and Mrs. George M. Kaufman made a special effort to facilitate my research, as did Florence Montgomery. David Barquist and Kim Sichel deserve a warm acknowledgment for their exceptionally devoted and intelligent participation in various capacities.

Many scholars and specialists extended themselves graciously in aiding my research. W. Scott Braznell provided me with an abundance of sources and suggestions, including the title of the exhibition, and gave a careful evaluation of a draft of the catalogue. Martin Eidelberg, J. Stewart Johnson, R. Craig Miller, Derek Ostergard, Dianne H. Pilgrim, and Susan Fillin Yeh assisted in locating key objects for the exhibition and were extremely thorough and perceptive readers of the catalogue in its early stage. Their suggestions for improving it were fundamental and too numerous to acknowledge individually in every instance. Others who shared their knowledge of the field include Frederick R. Brandt, Holliday T. Day, David Farmer, Paul V. Gardner, Neil Harris, Edmund P. Hogan, Penelope Hunter-Stiebel, Wilma Keyes, Carol Herselle Krinsky, Suzanne Lipschutz, Catherine Lynn, Mary Jean Madigan, Clark S. Marlor, Jeffrey L. Meikle, Alan Moss, Patricia O'Donnell, Alice Irma Prather-Moses, Rodris Roth, George W. Scherma, Vincent Scully, Linda Steigleder, and Diane Tepfer.

I am indebted to the staffs of several institutions: Joanne Polster, Doris Stowens, and Bonnie Thone of the American Craft Museum; Joy Cattanach of the Museum of Fine Arts, Boston; Glenda Galt, Kevin Stayton, and Christopher Wilk of The Brooklyn Museum; Nancy O. Merrill and David W. Steadman of The Chrysler Museum; Lillian Clagett, Lucy Commoner, Anne Dorfsman, Robert C. Kaufmann, Margaret Luchars, David Revere McFadden, Gillian Moss, Milton Sonday, and Jacquelyn Wong of the Cooper-Hewitt Museum; Dwight Lanmon, Jane Shadel Spillman, and William Warmus of The Corning Museum of Glass; David A. Hanks and Associates; Carla Martin of the Delaware Art Museum; Ross Anderson of the Everson Museum of Art; Burr Sebring of Gorham-Textron; Patricia Everett of Barbara Mathes Gallery; Alice Cooney Frelinghuysen, Jeanie James, Linda Lawson, Mary Lorincz, and Jean E. Mailey of The Metropolitan Museum of Art; Mary Suzor and Nancy L. Swallow of the Museum of Fine Arts, Springfield, Massachusetts; Ulysses G. Dietz of The Newark Museum; Wendy Christie and Darrel L. Sewell of the Philadelphia Museum of Art; Tania Barter and Ronnie L. Zakon of the Rhode Island School of Design Museum of Art; the Robert Schoelkopf Gallery; the Textile Conservation Workshop; Elizabeth Pratt Fox, William N. Hosley, Jr., and Gregory Hedberg of the Wadsworth Atheneum; the Washburn Gallery; and Mansfield Bascom of The Wharton Esherick Museum.

In connection with my research, I was privileged to speak with designers and their relatives, associ-ates, and patrons. I wish to acknowledge the gracious assistance of Mrs. Alfred H. Barr, Jr., Mrs. Maurice Benjamin, Diana Diederich Blake, Isabelle Crocé, Millia Davenport, Donald Deskey, Mr. and Mrs. William

H. Diederich, Mrs. Samuel Dushkin, Maurice Heaton, Nathan George Horwitt, Duny Katzman, Mr. and
Mrs. Lee Rohde, Mrs. James J. Rorimer, Lee Schoen, and Tessim Zorach.

All of the lenders to "At Home in Manhattan" were extraordinarily cooperative and generous in their
assistance. The support and encouragement of my husband Henry was essential to the completion of my
work. I owe my most profound debt of gratitude to Patricia E. Kane, who was an exemplary mentor and
friend during every phase of this project and to whom the following essays are dedicated.

KAREN DAVIES
Rose Herrick Jackson Fellow

CONTENTS

"At Home in Manhattan: Modern Decorative Arts, 1925 to the Depression" is the first exhibition in several decades to highlight the works of major American designers active in New York City during the late 1920s. Including eighty-one objects by forty-seven designers, this exhibition sheds new light on a largely forgotten era of American design. In the past fifteen years several exhibitions in Europe and America have brought the so-called Art Deco style to public attention, and numerous histories of design movements of the 1920s have appeared.[1] These endeavors, however, have focused primarily on European developments, whereas American designs of the period remain largely unexamined.

A few critics have recently begun considering the unique aspects of American design in the 1920s. In architectural studies Robert Venturi, Vincent Scully, Cervin Robinson, Rosemarie Bletter, and David Gebhard have examined the American skyscrapers and other commercial and domestic buildings of the era.[2] American decorative arts of the period require a similar aesthetic and historical reevaluation.

The designs in this exhibition represent a creative alternative to the conservatism that dominated American decorative arts during the 1920s. In the first years of the decade, America's contributions to innovative design had declined. The arts and crafts movement was no longer a major creative force; in fact, the movement had begun to fall out of favor before World War I. Although some arts and crafts designers continued to work throughout the 1920s, Gustav Stickley, one of the American movement's leading furniture manufacturers, went out of business in 1916, and Louis Comfort Tiffany retired from Tiffany Studios in 1919.[3]

In the early years of the decade, American and European taste in the decorative arts was primarily historicist and retrospective. Period-revival furnishings, copied from historical prototypes, dominated the American market. The colonial revival began in the late nineteenth century, and when the Metropolitan Museum of Art in New York opened its American Wing in 1924, public awareness of historic American styles increased. The market for colonial and Federal period reproductions expanded. In domestic interiors these American styles vied for popularity with English Tudor, Spanish baroque, and eighteenth-century French revival furnishings.[4]

Although organizations of modern decorative artists in several European centers held annual salons or periodic exhibitions where innovative designs could be seen, only a handful of showplaces in America specialized in modern objects, such as Rena Rosenthal's Austrian Workshop in New York City.[5] Modern Viennese design was also represented in New York City during the 1910s by the work of Paul T. Frankl and Joseph Urban, recent emigrants from Vienna, and by the Aschermann Studio, an interior decoration firm influenced by the Wiener Werkstätte.[6] World War I, however, disrupted contact with modern European developments in the decorative arts, and in the immediate postwar years prejudice against immigrants from German-speaking countries probably suppressed the Austrian influence;[7] nevertheless throughout the 1920s, Viennese design continued as the most important European model for modern American decorative arts.

A handful of American designers on the eastern seaboard worked independently of the dominant revival styles. Frederick Carder, at the Steuben Division of Corning Glass Works, was one of the few American glass designers to make the transition from Art Nouveau to the new aesthetic directions of the 1920s. Hunt Diederich exhibited his metalwork regularly at the Salon d'Automne in Paris during the 1910s

1
See, for instance, Yvonne Brunhammer, *Les Années "25": Collections du Musée des Arts Decoratifs* (Paris: Musée des Arts Decoratifs, 1966); Musée des Arts Décoratifs, Paris, *Les Années "25": Art Déco / Bauhaus / Stijl / Esprit Nouveau* (1966); Judith Applegate, *Art Deco* (New York: Finch College Museum of Art, 1970); Bevis Hillier, *Art Deco* (Minneapolis, Minn.: Minneapolis Institute of Arts, 1971); Martin Battersby, *The Decorative Twenties* (London: Studio Vista, 1969); and Klaus-Jürgen Sembach, *Into the Thirties—Style and Design 1927–1934* (London: Thames and Hudson, 1972).

2
See, for instance, Robert Venturi, *Complexity and Contradiction in Architecture* (New York: Museum of Modern Art, 1977, rev. ed.), with introduction by Vincent Scully; Cervin Robinson and Rosemarie Haag Bletter, *Skyscraper Style: Art Deco New York* (New York: Oxford University Press, 1975); David Gebhard and Harriette Von Breton, *Kem Weber: The Moderne in Southern California, 1920 through 1941* (Santa Barbara: The Art Galleries, University of California, 1969).

3
See Phyllis Ackerman, *Wallpaper: Its History, Design and Use* (New York: Frederick A. Stokes, 1923), 81, for a typically negative assessment of the arts and crafts movement in the 1920s.

4
"The Art Museum and the Store," *Good Furniture Magazine* 24 (March 1925): 142; Dudley Crafts Watson, *Interior Decoration* (Chicago: American Library Association, 1932), 16. The illustrations in Eugene Clute, *The Treatment of Interiors* (New York: Pencil Points Press, 1926), give evidence of the prevailing taste in reproduction styles during the period.

5
Rudolph Rosenthal and Helena L. Ratzka, *The Story of Modern Applied Art* (New York: Harper and Brothers, 1948), 169–70, 174. Rena Rosenthal's Austrian Workshop appears for the first time in R. L. Polk and Co.'s, *Trow New York Copartnership and Corporation Directory: Boroughs of Manhattan and Bronx* (New York), in 1916–17. By 1922 the establishment was called Rena Rosenthal Studio.

6
See Rebecca Van Houghton, "Modern Influences in Interior Decoration," *Town and Country* 70 (20 November 1915): 25–27, 50, 52. Source courtesy W. Scott Braznell.

and 1920s, and in 1922 he received a Gold Medal from the Architectural League of New York.[8] In 1923 Henry Varnum Poor gained immediate recognition from his first exhibition of ceramics at the Montross Gallery in New York City.[9] Carl Walters showed his pottery at the Whitney Studio Club in 1924, and from that exhibition one of his pieces was acquired by Gertrude Vanderbilt Whitney.[10] Both native-born and recently emigrated designers, such as Russel Wright, Norman Bel Geddes, Frankl, and Urban, found the New York theater world a fertile environment of experimentation early in the decade. These individuals were exceptional, however; most of the American designers who became important in the latter part of the decade had not begun working in modern styles or were receiving little recognition for their innovative creations before 1925.

This relatively unreceptive environment for modern design was due, in large part, to a lack of adventurous patrons or governmental subsidies. American designers producing modern work generally did not receive the private support behind such entrepreneurial ventures in Europe as the Wiener Werkstätte. The governmental funds that contributed to the operation of German design schools such as the Bauhaus were unparalleled in this country until the WPA art projects of the Depression era.[11]

The Paris "Exposition Internationale des Arts Décoratifs et Industriels Modernes" of 1925 dramatically increased awareness of modern European design in this country (cat. 1).[12] Months before its opening American journals mentioned it with anticipation. *The American Magazine of Art* reported:

> The United States will not be represented in the Exposition of Decorative and Industrial Art to be held in Paris next summer. The French Government offered us one of the best sites set aside for foreign countries and urged participation. Our Government took the matter under serious consideration and was in sympathy with the project. But we could not qualify [because] this exposition [will display] exclusively works which are modernistic in design; none which is based on tradition is to be included. In this way . . . the French propose to capture the trade of the world in this field.[13]

Herbert Hoover, then Secretary of Commerce, declined the French government's invitation by saying that America had nothing modern to show at the Exposition.[14] Hoover had overlooked America's contributions to modern architecture, but for the mainstream of decorative design he was correct.[15]

The Exposition revealed the isolation of the United States from progressive European design. Motivated by curiosity and the desire to become conversant with modern decorative arts, thousands of Americans visited the exhibition, and reports of the event were generally favorable. The French displays attracted the most attention; works by Emile-Jacques Ruhlmann (cat. 2), Edgar Brandt (cat. 3), and other Parisian designers received much praise. In addition to French designs, Scandinavian glass and decorative objects from Austria impressed visitors. Like their French counterparts, most European exhibitors submitted designs that relied on earlier decorative arts traditions. Entries most divorced from the past—Le Corbusier's L'Esprit Nouveau and the Russian pavilions—were not much noticed by American visitors or were dismissed as radical aberrations. Bauhaus objects were not exhibited because, for political reasons, Germany was invited too late to participate.[16]

Of course, some American observers were hostile to this startling exposure to modern design.

7
Kem Weber, a German immigrant living in California, felt a similar prejudice during these years that prevented him from working in a modern design mode. See Gebhard and Von Breton, *Kem Weber,* 38.

8
Detroit Institute of Arts, *Arts and Crafts in Detroit, 1906–1976: The Movement, The Society, The School* (Detroit, 1976), 92.

9
Ibid., 81.

10
Garth Clark, *A Century of Ceramics in the United States, 1878–1978* (New York: E. P. Dutton in association with the Everson Museum of Art, 1979), 338.

11
On European patronage of modern design, see Christopher Wilk, *Marcel Breuer: Furniture and Interiors* (New York: Museum of Modern Art, 1981), 35; Barbara Miller Lane, *Architecture and Politics in Germany, 1918–1945* (Cambridge, Mass.: Harvard University Press, 1968), 122–23; Penelope Hunter-Stiebel, *The Metropolitan Museum of Art Bulletin* 37 (Winter 1979–80): 14; John Loring, "American Deco," *The Connoisseur* 200 (January 1979): 48.

12
C. A. Glassgold, "Design in America," in R. L. Leonard and C. A. Glassgold, eds., *Annual of American Design 1931* (New York: Ives Washburn, 1930), 174.

13
"Modernism in Industrial Art," *American Magazine of Art* 15 (October 1924): 540.

14
Rosenthal and Raztka, *Modern Applied Art,* 174.

15
Leonard and Glassgold, *Annual of American Design 1931,* 133.

16
Robinson and Bletter, *Skyscraper Style,* 44.

Richardson Wright, editor of *House and Garden,* predicted, "It is very much doubted if the modernist movement, as applied to the home, ever gets a strong foothold in this country."[17] Many periodicals covered the exhibition with enthusiasm,[18] however, and in 1926 the Metropolitan Museum of Art displayed a selection of objects from the Exposition, providing further contact with novel European decorative arts in this country.[19]

"At Home in Manhattan" documents the period of renewed vitality in New York design circles following the Paris Exposition. Modern designers were working in Cleveland, Chicago, Los Angeles, and elsewhere, but according to contemporary assessments, Manhattan was "the nation's style pulse."[20] The exhibition's date span begins with 1925 and ends with the Depression, when by 1932 economic necessity and philosophical reorientation caused American design to undergo a fundamental aesthetic transformation. Reflecting New York's role as style center for the decorative arts, "At Home in Manhattan" presents works only by those designers who exhibited work or executed commissions in that city during the late 1920s. The focus on decorative arts for the home reflects the character of design exhibitions during the period. In the influential museum and department store displays of the late 1920s, the majority of objects shown were home furnishings; "At Home in Manhattan" follows these earlier precedents.

Although the designs presented here represent some of the best American work produced during the period, objects by some of the major figures of the era—Raymond Loewy, Waylande Gregory, Frederick Kiesler, Henrietta and Winold Reiss, Walter Kantack, William Lescaze, Marguerite Zorach, for example— were not located in time for inclusion in the exhibition. Frank Lloyd Wright received few commissions in the 1920s due to his personal notoriety and was viewed as more of a progenitor than a protagonist during these relatively inactive years of his career. Therefore he is featured only in the catalogue essay. The European objects in the exhibition are not a complete representation but suggest the kinds of imported designs that influenced the development of modern decorative arts in America during this period.

The American designers featured in this exhibition participated in, borrowed from, and modified current international developments in modern design. Characterized by wide-ranging eclecticism, American decorative arts of the late 1920s do not now have an adequate descriptive label. In our time these objects have been categorized as "Art Deco," "Zig-Zag Moderne," and "The Exposition Style," but these terms were not used in the 1920s.[21] Innovative French decorative arts were named *"art moderne"* during the period, and sometimes that label was applied to American pieces. More commonly, contemporaries referred to various new developments in the decorative arts as "modernistic" (especially if the designs involved cubistic forms) or simply "modern."

In the midst of a thoroughgoing aesthetic reevaluation in the late 1920s, most American observers had an elastic concept of what constituted modern design. They used "modern" to refer to various progressive developments rather than one set of fixed stylistic characteristics of a single school.[22] Throughout the 1930s, however, the term "modernism" became increasingly associated with the work of the German Bauhaus designers (cat. 74), Le Corbusier, and other individuals who evolved a design idiom that came to be known as the International Style. This functionalist mode was officially established in American intellectual circles as the uncontested expression of modernism by the early design exhibitions at the Museum of Modern Art and the writings of Philip Johnson, Henry-Russell Hitchcock, and others.[23] Very little

17
Richardson Wright, "The Modernist Taste," *House and Garden* 48 (October 1925): 78–79.
18
See, for instance, "The International Exposition of Modern Decorative and Industrial Art," *Good Furniture Magazine* 25 (September 1925): 121; Howell S. Cresswell, "The Paris Exposition of Modern Decorative Arts," *Good Furniture Magazine* 25 (October, December 1925): 187–97, 310–17; Georges Villa, "Paris Exposition Shows Way to New Art of Future," *American Magazine of Art* 17 (April 1926): 190–92.
19
Nellie C. Sanford, "The Loan Exhibition from the Paris Exposition Shown in The Metropolitan Museum of Art," *Good Furniture Magazine* 26 (April 1926): 185–88.
20
"New York—The Nation's Style Pulse," *Retailing* 1 (13 April 1929): 17.

21
See Jeffrey L. Meikle, *Twentieth Century Limited: Industrial Design in America, 1925–1939* (Philadelphia: Temple University Press, 1979), xiii, for a discussion of recent stylistic terminology.
22
Critics of the period, however, sometimes developed categories within the parameters of modern design based on the use of, or independence from, tradition. See, for instance, Katharine Morrison Kahle, *Modern French Decoration* (New York: G. P. Putnam's Sons, 1930), 36, and Thérèse and Louise Bonney, *Buying Antique and Modern Furniture in Paris* (New York: Robert M. McBride, 1929), 28. Sources courtesy J. Stewart Johnson.
23
Henry-Russell Hitchcock, Jr., *Modern Architecture: Romanticism and Reintegration* (New York: Payson & Clarke, 1929); Hitchcock and Philip Johnson, et al., *Modern Architecture: International Exhibition* (New York: Museum of Modern Art, 1932). See also Richard Horn, "MOMA's 'Good Design' Programs Changed Historic U.S. Taste," *Industrial Design* 29 (March–April 1982): 43–44; Gebhard and Von Breton, *Kem Weber,* 6.

American work of the 1920s was produced in this rigorous functionalist idiom. In retrospect, American design was therefore dismissed as rear guard and unworthy of the designation "modernist."

Today, however, we are experiencing another phase of aesthetic reorientation in an era increasingly known as "post-modern." Since the 1960s Venturi and other critics have called into question the definition of modernism and have argued for more pluralistic criteria in evaluating both contemporary design and work from the past.[24] The following essays use the term "modern" in this pluralistic, inclusive sense, more to denote objects conceived in the progressive spirit of the late 1920s rather than to imply an unvarying set of stylistic characteristics.

Instead of coining new labels for the varied aspects of 1920s decorative arts, this publication presents the objects in five thematic categories based on the diversity of American design during the era. "Using the Past" explores the ways in which designers incorporated tradition into modern decorative arts. "Modern Art" discusses the influence of twentieth-century painting, sculpture, and architecture on decorative design during the period. "Urban Life" presents examples of the appropriation of city imagery into objects produced for domestic use. "Promoting Modern Design" deals with the exhibitions, organizations, and publications that introduced the public to new developments in the decorative arts. "Design for Industry" focuses on the beginnings of the industrial design profession and objects that relate to major aesthetic changes of the 1930s.

Inevitably these thematic categories overlap. An object such as Walter von Nessen's "Diplomat" coffee service (cat. 80) could satisfy the criteria of no fewer than four categories. Similarly, designs by a single artist are found in more than one category; Paul T. Frankl's work appears in three. The divisions are not arbitrary, however: in every case various factors were weighed and the categorization was dictated by how well each object explicates the major influences of the time.

Although American design of this period strongly relied on Europe, "At Home in Manhattan" is not exclusively concerned with stylistic transmission between the United States and the Continent. A complete investigation of all the possible design sources for each object was not possible; in some cases close European prototypes may exist, and much research remains for other students of American design.

This exhibition aims to diverge from the critical bias that judges American decorative arts of this period almost exclusively (and often unfavorably) in terms of contemporary European work. This bias was felt when the designers represented were still active. In 1938 Russel Wright attended the Museum of Modern Art's exhibition of Bauhaus design and was offended by an admirer of German functionalism who derided contemporary American design in comparison. Wright responded:

Why can't someone, a Museum of Modern Art or a New York World's Fair, put on an exhibit in which they would dramatize all design that is American? First, let them parade those unconscious developments, free from any aesthetic inferiority complexes. Our bridges. Our roads. Our factory machinery. Our skyscrapers. Let them throw a spotlight on our shining bathrooms and our efficient kitchens. Roll out our trick cocktail gadgets—our streamlined iceboxes—our streamlined pencil sharpeners. . . . Let them put a magnifying glass (if they feel they need it) over these things to find the American character. . . . Let them do this without recourse to European standards in their

24
Venturi, *Complexity and Contradiction in Architecture,* 1977 ed., 13–16.

selection. It has never been done. But I know that they will find that there is a distinct American character of design in all that is American and that our home furnishings *tie in to this character.* Not until then, will we know of what elements this American character consists.[25]

Although not advocating an examination of American developments in isolation, this exhibition has tried to respond to Wright's demands.

The objects in "At Home in Manhattan" provide valuable insights into a tremendously vital and experimental period in New York's history. As one perceptive observer wrote in 1928: "Style is a manifestation of an attitude toward life. It serves to chronicle a period as effectively as written history."[26] In essence, the objects assembled here tell us much about the ways American designers appropriated tradition, technology, modern art, and their changing urban environment into new and creative designs.

25
Quoted in Martin Greif, *Depression Modern: The Thirties Style in America* (New York: Universe Books, 1975), 43.

26
Helen Appleton Read, "Twentieth-Century Decoration," *Vogue* 71 (1 April 1928):134. Source courtesy W. Scott Braznell.

Notes to the Catalogue Entries

The objects in the exhibition were chosen
to be as representative as possible of their
original condition. Any exceptions to this
criterion are noted in the entries.

Objects are unmarked unless otherwise
indicated.

In the furniture entries, the description of
materials lists primary woods before sec-
ondary woods; these categories are sepa-
rated by a semicolon.

Regarding dates of objects, "about" indicates that evidence exists for assigning a
date close to the one indicated. "Circa"
indicates that the object probably dates
from within five years of the date given.

Abbreviations have been used as follows:
H. for height; W. for width; L. for length;
D. for depth; DIAM. for diameter; WT. for
weight; dwt. for pennyweight.

1 Poster

"Exposition Internationale des Arts Décoratifs et Industriels Modernes," 1925
Designed by Robert Bonfils (1886–1972), printed by Imprimerie de Vaugirard, Paris
Colored lithograph on paper
H. 45¼ in. (120 cm), w. 29½ in. (50 cm)
Signed (in the plate) center left, "Robert bonfils"; marked (in the plate) center bottom,
"IMPRIMERIE DE VAUGIRARD, PARIS"
Collection of John Axelrod,
Boston, Massachusetts

Called a "cubist dream city" by one visitor,[1] the 1925 Paris "Exposition Internationale des Arts Décoratifs et Industriels Modernes" stimulated a new interest in modern design in this country. Plans for the exhibition began as early as 1911 by Parisian organizations of decorative artists, including the Société des artistes décorateurs, whose idealistic goals were similar to those of other modern movements in Europe. They aimed to resolve the conflict between art and industry, to merge the status of artist and artisan, and to raise the quality of mass-produced objects.[2] Postponed by World War I, the exhibition evolved into a grand international project sponsored by the French government. Most of the deluxe objects in the exhibition from France and other European countries were meticulously hand crafted; relatively few mass-produced objects were included.

This poster, by the French artist Robert Bonfils, also a designer of fabrics and tapestries,[3] uses several of the motifs asso-ciated with French decorative arts of the period: female figures surrounded by gazelles, baskets of stylized roses, and backgrounds of flattened, two-dimensional plant forms or fountains.

1
Helen Appleton Read, "The Exposition in Paris," *International Studio* 82 (November 1925): 96.
2
"Origines de la Exposition des Arts Décoratifs et Industriels Modernes," in Imprimerie Nationale, Office Central d'Editions et de Librairie, *Encyclopédie des arts décoratifs et industriels modernes au XXème siècle* (Paris, 1925; reprint, New York: Garland, 1977), 1:20. Philippe Garner, *Twentieth-Century Furniture* (New York: Van Nostrand Reinhold, 1980), 68; Bevis Hillier, *Art Deco of the 20s and 30s* (London: Studio Vista, 1968), 13.
3
Kahle, *Modern French Decoration,* 127.

Corner Cabinet

about 1916

Designed by Emile-Jacques Ruhlmann
(1879–1933), Paris, France

Macassar ebony and ivory

H. 50½ in. (128.3 cm), w. 33½ in. (85.1 cm),
D. 23¾ in. (60.3 cm)

Collection of Sydney and Frances Lewis

The leading cabinetmaker in France during
this period, Emile-Jacques Ruhlmann first
exhibited at the Salon d'Automne in 1913
and established his own workshop after
World War I. A sumptuous creation from
this establishment could take up to 1,200
hours to produce.[1] This three-legged corner cabinet is representative of the pieces
by Ruhlmann that Americans so greatly
admired at the 1925 Paris Exposition. The
Metropolitan Museum of Art commissioned a similar design to this one with four
legs instead of three.

The ivory inlay representing a basket
of flowers and the exotic veneers on this
piece epitomize the kind of deluxe objects
produced by Ruhlmann and some of his
French colleagues during this period.
Although ornate by twentieth-century
standards, the design is much more
restrained than the ormolu-encrusted
works of eighteenth-century French cabinetmakers that served as Ruhlmann's
models. He extracted certain essential
ideas from these earlier traditions but was
influenced by the aesthetics of his own
time, unlike furniture makers working in
period-revival styles. When installed in the
Metropolitan Museum of Art's gallery of
contemporary decorative arts, Ruhlmann's
striking designs converted many Americans to an appreciation of modern decorative art.

1
Brunhammer, *Les Années "25,"* 70; Aaron
Sheon, "Lucien Rollin, Architecte-Décora-
teur of the 1930s," *Arts Magazine* 56 (May
1982):111.

3 Fireplace Screen

about 1924

Executed by Edgar Brandt (1880–1960),
Paris, France

Wrought iron

H. 36¹¹⁄₁₆ in. (93.2 cm),
w. 30¼ in. (76.8 cm),
D. 10¾ in. (27.3 cm)

Stamped on front, upper right corner,
"MADE IN FRANCE E. BRANDT"

Yale University Art Gallery, 1981.2

Edgar Brandt was one of the best-known
modern French designers in this country
during the late 1920s. Several of his
designs came to the United States with the
traveling exhibition of works from the 1925
Paris Exposition, including a version of this
fire screen. A set of iron doors executed in
1925 for Cheney Brothers, a textile company with offices on Madison Avenue,
New York City, also enhanced Brandt's
reputation in this country. The geometricized, two-dimensional floral ornamentation on these doors inspired much modern
architectural decoration in America. In
1926 the company published *The Romance of Design*, reproducing this screen
design on its cover.[1] The object was most
likely sold in America through Ferrobrandt,
Inc., the artist's New York retail outlet.

1
Garnet Warren and Horace B. Cheney,
The Romance of Design (Garden City,
N.Y.: Doubleday, Page, 1926).

USING THE PAST

The objects in this section simultaneously reflect the influence of traditional decorative arts and maintain integrity as modern designs. Created by formal simplification and imaginative adaptation of historical models, these objects were never conceived as period reproductions. The artists who produced them were familiar with the use of historical models through contact with various modern design movements in Europe. American designers, like their European counterparts, recreated the forms of past traditions using a contemporary, progressive idiom.

Modern American designers of the 1920s were eclectic yet selective in their use of historical models. Some designs, such as Erik Magnussen's tea service (cat. 14), synthesize several different modern and traditional sources into one ensemble. The designers of the era inherited this eclecticism from their nineteenth-century predecessors, who selected and freely combined stylistic features from many different sources. In the 1920s, however, modern designers rejected the exuberant historical revival styles of the nineteenth century, which had come to epitomize the ultimate "bad" taste in interior decor.[1] The best designers integrated an awareness of historical models into aesthetic statements distinctly appropriate to their own age.

Because these designs overtly refer to tradition, they form a category of modern work independent of the functionalist principles developed but never dominant in Europe during the 1920s. The vanguard theories of the German Bauhaus designers, Le Corbusier, and other adherents to the International Style proposed that the forms of inexpensively mass-produced, utilitarian objects should reflect their purposes, materials, and manufacturing processes. According to these theories, nonessential or historically derived ornament compromised design purity,[2] and luxury objects were considered socially irresponsible. Breaking decisively with the past, Bauhaus designers, such as Marcel Breuer, evolved revolutionary concepts in furniture design (cat. 74). He wrote in a 1927 essay titled "metal möbel", "Our work is unrelenting and unretrospective; it despises tradition and established custom."[3]

The functionalist principles underlying the most antitraditional architecture and design in Europe during this period were not rigorously followed by the majority of designers in America, although Richard Neutra and Rudolph Schindler produced International Style buildings in California. Functionalist theories were known among certain members of the New York intelligentsia,[4] but most American designers at this time worked in isolation from the International Style and produced objects closer to the ornate and historically referential designs of the Wiener Werkstätte and deluxe furniture makers in Paris.

Much of the modern French furniture produced during the 1920s relied heavily on tradition and often reinterpreted Louis XVI and Empire styles.[5] The work of Emile-Jacques Ruhlmann exemplifies the creative reuse of tradition in the majority of the furniture seen at the Paris Exposition. His palatial pavilion was an all-out effort to recapture the splendor and refinement of eighteenth-century aristocratic interiors. He emulated the elaborate techniques of ivory inlay and exotic veneers (cat. 2) developed by predecessors such as Jean-Henri Riesener, one of the official cabinetmakers to Louis XVI.[6] Although relying on tradition as a point of departure, Ruhlmann's furniture seemed extremely modern to American viewers.

In the wake of the 1925 Paris Exposition, growing interest in modern decorative arts generated commissions for designers in New York City, but circumstances prevented widespread adoption of the French mode. Although sharing a reliance on tradition with most European furniture makers, designers in

1
See press release, M. W. Colwell, "Data on Exposition of Bad Taste," 19 April 1914, in the collection of Wilma Keyes. The document announces the "Exposition of Bad Taste or the Casket of Domestic Fine Art," held in 1914 at the Modernist Studios, New York City, which lampooned such Victorian objects as a reproduction of the Venus de Milo with a clock in her stomach. The jury included Elsie de Wolfe, Frank Crowninshield, and others.

2
John McAndrew, " 'Modernistic' and 'Streamlined'," *Museum of Modern Art Bulletin* 5 (December 1938): 2–3.

3
Quoted in Wilk, *Breuer,* 69.

4
Maurice Heaton recalls that Bauhaus theories were enthusiastically discussed among members of the Architectural League of New York in the late 1920s. Maurice Heaton to author, conversation, 22 January 1983. Le Corbusier's *Towards a New Architecture* was published in English in 1927, and Edwin A. Park, in *New Backgrounds for a New Age* (New York: Harcourt, Brace, 1927), 94–96, speaks approvingly of Le Corbusier's theoretical tracts. In addition, the avant-garde journal *Little Review* sponsored a "Machine Age Exposition" that featured the work of Walter Gropius and other International Style architects. See *Little Review, Machine Age Exposition* (New York, 1927): 25–27.

5
Ackerman, *Wallpaper,* 83, 85.

6
Sheon, "Lucien Rollin," 111; Patricia Bayer, ed., *The Fine Art of the Furniture Maker* (Rochester, N.Y.: Memorial Art Gallery of the University of Rochester, 1981), 98.

this country lacked many of the essential prerequisites for producing luxurious objects, especially in comparison with their French counterparts. American designers did not share the specific incentive of the French to recapture their renowned eighteenth-century craft tradition and had limited access to the range of skills and exotic materials available in Paris. In addition, the opulent formality of modern French furnishings, scaled to the grand apartments of Paris, was somewhat inappropriate to the smaller rooms in most American homes.

American adaptations of modern French furniture generally appealed to a very restricted and affluent clientele. Patrons either commissioned close copies of French designs or obtained imported furnishings from Paris. Jules Bouy, who arrived in this country from Belgium around the time of World War I, provided several fashionable apartments with Parisian furnishings; his own interior designs closely followed the tradition-inspired styles of the Paris Exposition. Louis Rorimer also designed furnishings close to French models, such as cat. 7. The dining table's U-shaped support on a pedestal base was a common feature in contemporary French design, deriving from Empire consoles with lyre-shaped pedestals.

During this period Eugene Schoen was often described as an American designer who worked in the French idiom. According to one writer: "[Schoen] adapted to American tastes the best features of the French mode—the use of fine woods, beautiful inlays, [and] sweeping, highly polished surfaces."[7] Schoen's furniture (cat. 6) was sometimes inspired by contemporary French designs but relied more on geometric arrangements of wood grain than on applied ornament.[8] His use of veneers on large case pieces was actually closer to German and Viennese conventions of cabinetmaking. In keeping with French traditions, however, each of his works was individually made, unique in some of its details, and quite costly. Schoen had his designs executed at Schmieg, Hungate and Kotzian, a New York firm that specialized in quality revival furnishings and had access to exotic woods.[9]

In addition to the interest in eighteenth-century cabinetmaking, many American objects of the 1920s reflected an awareness and appreciation of neoclassicism. The resurgence of neoclassicism during this period was the result of European and American painters, sculptors, and designers searching for formal prototypes with restrained and clearly defined forms. The historical associations of the classical tradition were relatively unimportant to designers of the 1920s; they tended to simplify classical ornament to a greater extent than their nineteenth-century predecessors, influenced by the rise of abstraction in all the arts. Walter von Nessen, who was born in Germany and worked in Sweden before coming to the United States in 1923, was strongly influenced by this mode. The crowning urn on his mirror (cat. 4) is adapted from a neoclassical motif commonly used at the turn of the nineteenth century. Peter Müller-Munk, who arrived in this country from Germany shortly after the Paris Exposition, also reinterpreted in his silverwork the late eighteenth- and early nineteenth-century neoclassical tradition (cat. 9).

American designers, like their European counterparts, also looked to exotic sources for formal models and lacquerwork techniques. Oriental design provided the inspiration for Paul Frankl's mirror (cat. 16), Peter Müller-Munk's silver bowl (cat. 18), and the etched glass vessel by Frederick Carder (cat. 19). Reflecting an interest in bold, two-dimensional graphic patterns, American designers also explored Egyptian, Mesopotamian, archaic Greek, Middle Eastern, and American Indian craft traditions for visual sources of abstract forms and animal motifs. The grazing goats depicted on an ancient Rhodian vase (fig.

7
Nellie C. Sanford, "An Architect-Designer of Modern Furniture," *Good Furniture Magazine* 30 (March 1928):116–17.
8
Compare, for instance, a Ruhlmann cabinet illustrated in Clute, *Treatment of Interiors,* 103, with Schoen's buffet (cat. 6).

9
Sanford, "Architect-Designer," 117–18.

Figure 2.
Black-figured Oinochoë.
Rhodian, sixth century B.C.
Photograph courtesy The Metropolitan
Museum of Art.

2) are typical of the designs that might have inspired the ibexes on Hunt Diederich's chandelier and bowl (cats. 21, 23). Ilonka and Mariska Karasz's embroidery (cat. 27) reinterprets Eastern European craft traditions, and the wall hanging by Lydia Bush-Brown (cat. 28) relates to textiles of the Middle East.

Modern appropriations of ancient craft and folk traditions were not new developments in the 1920s. Nineteenth-century designers incorporated vernacular traditions into their work and were fascinated with the symbolism of artifacts from preindustrial craft societies. Although modern designers in the 1920s continued to look to primitive and archaic forms for artistic inspiration, they generally lacked the nineteenth-century interest in vernacular artifacts as a key to understanding rapidly disappearing indigenous cultures. Ely Jacques Kahn, one of the period's most articulate designers, wrote: "We tend to go into raptures over certain primitive forms and to adopt them bodily as patterns without taking the trouble to discover the character of the design or the spirit that developed the design. The fact that some native form may be a religious symbol means nothing whatsoever to us."[10] Designers had been taught by the aesthetics of cubism, fauvism, and other avant-garde movements to see vernacular crafts as primarily formal models, and therefore they disregarded symbolic content to a greater degree than had their nineteenth-century predecessors.

Above all, vernacular models attracted modern designers because certain craft traditions seemed to relate aesthetically to new design innovations. Native American rugs and pottery were found to harmonize with the latest chromium and Bakelite furnishings; a formal similarity between ancient and modern art legitimated the juxtaposition of traditional Indian handcrafts with machine-made objects.[11] Modern designs derived from folk sources, such as Ilonka and Mariska Karasz's embroidery (cat. 27), even appeared in settings designed to promote the machine aesthetic, such as Kem Weber's installation at the 1931 exhibition of the American Union of Decorative Artists and Craftsmen. With few exceptions American designers were not opposed to reproducing folk-derived forms with modern machine techniques. In fact they saw this combination of old and new as a synthesis of primitive vitality and machine-age sophistication.[12]

American designers continued synthesizing past and present in their work well into the Depression decade. In their writings, they expressed enthusiasm for life in the machine age. Similar to the spirit behind the period-revival styles of the 1920s, however, the modern designers' search for aesthetic models was retrospective and wide ranging. Chinese bronzes, Rhodian pottery, and Empire console tables were only a few of their sources; this retrospective eclecticism in both conservative and progressive design circles indicates a lack of confidence in contemporary American culture as a source of artistic inspiration.

Modern American designers of the 1920s, however, were not seeking to restore the past through their use of historical prototypes but had an appropriate respect for the traditions that inspired them. This respect for the usefulness of the past gradually disappeared in modern design circles of the 1930s. Since then a generation of modernists have disregarded tradition, and although some of today's decorative artists are returning to historical models for inspiration,[13] the question still remains whether the past will again become integrated into contemporary design.

10
Ely Jacques Kahn, *Design in Art and Industry* (New York: Charles Scribner's Sons, 1935), 35–36.

11
"Indian Craftwork for Our Homes," *Good Furniture Magazine* 32 (April 1929): 216–17.

12
Ruth Reeves, "Relation of Modernism to Linen," *Retailing* 1 (5 January 1929):19; M. D. C. Crawford, "Primitive Art and Modern Design," *Creative Art* 3 (December 1928): xliv.

13
Notably, the recent work of Wendell Castle. See illustration, *Art in America* 71 (March 1983), inside front cover.

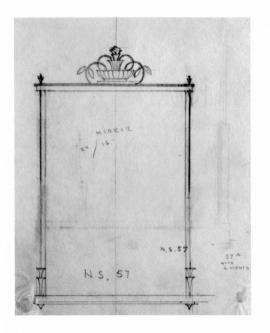

4 Wall Mirror
about 1930
Designed by Walter von Nessen
(1889–1943)
for Nessen Studio, Inc., New York City
Pewter, brass, and glass
H. 20 in. (50.8 cm), w. 17¾ in. (45.1 cm)
Stamped on back of urn, "N 42"
Alan Moss Studios, New York City

5 Design for Mirror
about 1930
Designed by Walter von Nessen for
Nessen Studio, Inc., New York City
Pencil on tracing paper
H. 9⅝ in. (24.5 cm), w. 7⅛ in. (18.1 cm)
(irregular)
Inscribed on front, "MIRROR/29/16/N.S.
57/57 A WITH 2 LIGHTS"
Alan Moss Studios, New York City

Walter von Nessen was born in Germany and studied in Berlin with Bruno Paul, an important educator and furniture designer.[1] Before immigrating to this country in 1923, von Nessen redesigned the interiors of the Berlin subway stations, taught at the Charlottenburg Art School, and spent from 1919 to 1923 in Stockholm, Sweden, designing furniture.[2] In the mid-1920s he established Nessen Studio in New York City, a company that supplied architects and interior designers with innovative light fixtures and metal furnishings. Eliel Saarinen used von Nessen's lamps (cat. 59) for the interiors of the Cranbrook Academy of Art in Bloomfield Hills, Michigan.

This mirror may reflect von Nessen's contact with Swedish designers working in a neoclassical vein.[3] The design adapts the crowning urns that often appeared on mirrors at the turn of the nineteenth century. The flaring ornaments at the bottom of the rods resemble highly abstracted lotus blossoms, a decorative form used in the early twentieth century by Austrian designers associated with the Wiener Werkstätte, such as Koloman Moser.[4]

The mirror is quite close to the preparatory drawing. The designer has worked out on paper different options for the length, proportions, and ornamentation. The version of the mirror pictured in this drawing appeared in a 1930 advertisement for Nessen Studio.[5] "N.S. 57" indicates a Nessen Studio catalogue number.

1
Who's Who in American Art, 1936–37, s.v. "von Nessen, Walter."
2
Obituary, *New York Times,* 5 September 1943, p. 28.
3
Compare a 1922 pewter mirror designed by Nils Fougstedt, in Nils G. Wollin, *Modern Swedish Decorative Art* (London: Architectural Press, 1931), 66.
4
Compare illustration in Christian Meyer, *Kolo Moser, Painter and Designer, 1868–1918* (Vienna: Galerie Metropol, 1983), 14–16.
5
See illustration in *House and Garden* 58 (December 1930): 21. Source courtesy W. Scott Braznell.

6 Buffet and Base

1927

Designed by Eugene Schoen (1880–1957)
for Eugene Schoen, Inc.,
executed by Schmieg, Hungate and
Kotzian, New York City

Walnut, bubinga, imbua burl,
macassar ebony, and rosewood; oak

H. 36 in. (91.4 cm), w. 82 in. (208.3 cm),
D. 24 in. (61 cm)

Philadelphia Museum of Art,
Gift of the Modern Club of Philadelphia.
29–45–1

A native New Yorker, Eugene Schoen
received a degree in architecture from
Columbia University in 1901, and upon
graduation won a scholarship to travel in
Europe where he met Otto Wagner and
Josef Hoffmann.[1] Schoen established an
architectural practice in New York City in
1905, and after seeing the 1925 Paris
Exposition he was inspired to set up an
interior decoration service. He operated a
gallery (cat. 71) that sold imported items
and his own designs for textiles and furniture.[2] His design firm attracted numerous
commissions for apartment interiors,
banks, theaters, and department stores in
Manhattan and elsewhere.

Schoen's furniture, with its exotic
veneers and neoclassical proportions,
relates to luxury cabinetmaking in several
national traditions. The arrangement of
veneers on this buffet is similar to contemporary German work and is especially
close to the case pieces of Viennese
designers such as Fritz Gross.[3] The mas-
siveness of this buffet is unusual in
Schoen's oeuvre, but practicality determined its commodious size. With a typically modern distaste for Victorian clutter,
Schoen designed this object to conceal as
much of the dining-room eating parapher-
nalia as possible.[4] When the buffet entered
the Philadelphia Museum's collection in
1929, curator Joseph Downs called it "the
finest piece of furniture made by an American craftsman in the modern manner."[5]

1
Lee Schoen, the son of Eugene Schoen, to
author, letter, 15 February 1983. Lee
Schoen was a partner in his father's architectural firm beginning in the late 1920s.
2
Marya Mannes, "Gallery Notes," *Creative
Art* 2 (February 1928): XIII.
3
Compare a cupboard by Gross illustrated
in Geoffrey C. Holme and Shirley B. Wainwright, eds., *Decorative Art 1929* (New
York: Albert and Charles Boni, 1929), 134.
4
Eugene Schoen, "House and Garden's
Modern House," *House and Garden* 55
(February 1929): 94.
5
Joseph Downs, "A Buffet in the Contemporary Style," *Pennsylvania Museum Bulletin* 24 (March 1929): 19.

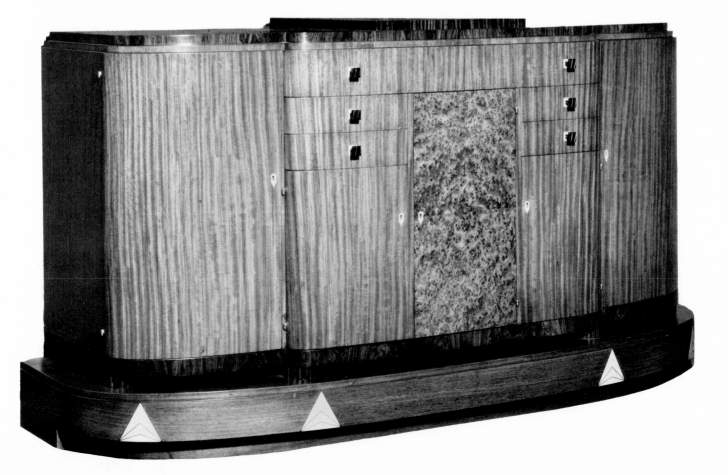

7 Dining Table
1927
Designed by Louis Rorimer (1872–1939),
executed by Rorimer Brooks Studios,
Cleveland, Ohio
Circassian walnut, ebonized and silvered
wood, aluminum, and brass-plated metal;
walnut, oak, and maple
Open: H. 29¼ in. (74.3 cm),
w. 90⅛ in. (228.9 cm),
D. 27⅞ in. (70.8 cm).
Closed: w. 50 in. (127 cm)
Collection of Louise Rorimer Dushkin

Louis Rorimer received art training at the
Manual Training School in his native city of
Cleveland. In the 1890s he studied abroad
at the Kunstgewerbeschüle in Munich and
in Paris at the Ecole des Arts Décoratifs

and the Académie Julien. His varied career
as artist, teacher, and businessman (he
was president of Rorimer Brooks Studios,
an interior design and furniture-making
firm) brought him wide recognition and
numerous commissions. Rorimer was a
member of the Hoover commission that
visited and reported on the 1925 Paris
Exposition. He designed residences
throughout the United States as well as
interiors for the Statler Hotel chain.[1] Rorimer was also a member of a professional
organization in New York, the American
Union of Decorative Artists and Craftsmen.

The table's elegant proportions, U-
shaped pedestal, and exotic woods relate
to furniture by Emile-Jacques Ruhlmann
and other French designers.[2] Belonging to
an ensemble of furnishings made for the
New York apartment of the artist's son and
daughter, James J. and Louise Rorimer, this

piece was adjusted to the scale of an unu-
sually small dining alcove. When fully
extended, the table seats eight diners; with
its leaves in place, it resembles a console
table. The aluminum bands on the pedestal protect the wood surfaces in the same
way that ormolu functioned on eighteenth-
century French furniture.[3]

1
Obituary, *New York Times,* 1 December
1939, p. 23.
2
Compare the supports on a table by Ruhlmann, illustrated in Imprimerie Nationale,
Office Central d'Editions, *Encyclopédie
des arts décoratifs et industriels modernes,*
4: pl. VI.
3
Observation courtesy Derek Ostergard.

8 Finger Bowl, Finger Bowl Plate, Goblet, Wine Glass, and Plate
"St. Tropez" pattern, 1932
Designed by Walter Dorwin Teague (1883–1960) for Steuben Division, Corning Glass Works, Corning, New York
Engraved colorless lead glass
Finger bowl, H. 3 in. (7.6 cm), DIAM. 3⅞ in. (9.8 cm)
Finger bowl plate, DIAM. 6¹⁵/₁₆ in. (17.6 cm)
Goblet, H. 6¾ in. (17.1 cm), DIAM. of rim 2⅞ in. (7.3 cm)
Wine glass, H. 5⅝ in. (14.3 cm), DIAM. of rim 3⅛ in. (8 cm)
Plate, DIAM. 8½ in. (21.6 cm)
Engraved on undersides in cursive script, "Steuben"; 8½ in. plate unmarked
The Brooklyn Museum, H. Randolph Lever Fund. 72.40.18a & b, .21, .22, .23

After studying at the Art Students League, Walter Dorwin Teague began working in 1908 in the art department of Calkins and Holden, an advertising agency in New York City. In the 1910s he was attracted to neoclassical forms in his study of eighteenth-century French culture. He visited Europe in 1926, where he saw the architecture of Le Corbusier, Walter Gropius, and Robert Mallet-Stevens. On returning to New York, he began working on a project in 1927 to redesign the cameras and showroom of the Eastman Kodak Company, a commission that established his reputation as an industrial designer.[1] In February 1932 Amory Houghton, then president of Corning Glass Works, hired Teague to help reverse the company's diminishing profits due to the Depression. Teague worked under contract for one year developing a modern line of colorless crystal tableware and decorative glass, a major shift from the earlier frosted and colored glass produced by the company.[2]

Teague's involvement with Steuben went farther than merely being a design consultant. With his advertising background, he analyzed the company's sales and production problems and recommended an image-conscious promotional campaign to establish the ownership of Steuben glassware as a sign of status.[3] Consequently the names of his designs have class-conscious appeal, and "St. Tropez" especially suggests the opulent resorts of the French Riviera. A Steuben sales catalogue of the 1930s declares that the simplicity and classic proportions of the "St. Tropez" pattern are "a contribution to modern art . . . perfectly suited to its purposes."[4]

Steuben, the Fostoria Glass Company, and other American glass manufacturers followed the lead of Scandinavian and Austrian companies, such as Orrefors and J. and L. Lobmeyr, and French glass designers like René Lalique and Jean Luce, and produced colorless engraved tableware for the modern dining room. These plates and glasses were often placed on glass tabletops or other surfaces that reflected their elegant, transparent forms.[5]

1
Mary Siff, "A Realist in Industrial Design," *Arts & Decoration* 41 (October 1934): 46–47; Meikle, *Twentieth Century Limited*, 43–46.
2
Mary Jean Smith Madigan, *Steuben Glass: An American Tradition in Crystal* (New York: Harry N. Abrams, 1982), 69.
3
Ibid., 69–70.
4
Steuben Glass, *Masterpieces in Glass by Steuben* (Corning, N.Y., n.d.), 9–10.
5
See, for instance, *Country Life* (U.S.) 65 (March 1934): 66. Paul V. Gardner, *The Glass of Frederick Carder* (New York: Crown Publishers, 1971), 321, for a line drawing of the "St. Tropez" pattern, no. 7485/T-31, from the 1932 Steuben catalogue. The prefix "T" indicates a Teague design (ibid., 100).

9 Coffee Service
(Pot, Creamer, and Sugar Bowl), 1927
Designed and executed by
Peter Müller-Munk (1904–1967),
New York City
Sterling silver, gold, and ebony
Pot, H. 7¼ in. (18.3 cm)
Creamer, H. 2⁷⁄₁₆ in. (6.2 cm)
Sugar bowl, H. 2⅞ in. (7.2 cm)
Total gross WT. 27 oz. 2 dwt. (843 gms)
Marked on undersides, "P [encircled]/
STERLING SILVER/925/1000"
Private Collection

Peter Müller-Munk was born in Germany,
studied at the University of Berlin, and
trained at the Kunstgewerbeschüle in Berlin with Waldemar Rämisch, a noted German silversmith. He immigrated to the
United States in 1926. Shortly after his
arrival he briefly designed for Tiffany and
Company but soon established his own
studio.[1] The Depression severely dimin-
ished the American market for custom-
made silver, and Müller-Munk moved into
the industrial design profession in the early
1930s.[2]

    In the late 1920s Müller-Munk was
not opposed to machine-produced silver
designs but maintained that the finest
metalwork was always handcrafted.[3] He
shared Raemisch's interest in reviving
ancient techniques of silver production and
believed that "based on old traditions, a
modern spirit can create a new art which
may last as did the masterpieces of the
past."[4]

    In this service the cylindrical bodies,
abstracted leaves encircling the bases,
and the pot's angular spout have prece-

dents in neoclassical silver, but Müller-
Munk has elongated the proportions for
greater vertical emphasis. The appliqué
borders of silver and gold leaves and the
ebony handles give the objects a precious
quality comparable to French work. The
quarter-circle handles on the sugar bowl
are a feature peculiar to German and
Scandinavian silver design of the period.[5]

1
Who's Who in American Art, 1947, s.v.
"Müller-Munk, Peter"; Augusta Owen Patterson, "The Decorative Arts," *Town and
Country* 83 (15 April 1928): 71; Helen
Appleton Read, "The Modern Theme Finds
a Distinctive Medium in American Silver,"
Vogue 72 (1 July 1928): 98. Sources courtesy W. Scott Braznell.
2
In The American Federation of Arts, *American Art Annual:* "Directory of Craftsmen
and Designers" (Washington, D.C., 1930),
553, Müller-Munk lists himself as a silversmith and an industrial designer.
3
Peter Müller-Munk, "Machine—Hand,"
Creative Art 5 (October 1929): 709–12.
4
Peter Müller-Munk, "Handwrought Silver,"
Charm 9 (April 1928): 83.
5
Compare illustration of a silver coffee service by the Swedish designer Nils Fougstedt
in Wollin, *Modern Swedish Decorative Art,*
94. For an illustration of Müller-Munk's
service on an ebony tray, see Müller-
Munk, "Handwrought Silver," 39.

10 Desk Set
(Blotter, Penholder, Letter Opener,
Cigarette Box with Insert),
about 1931
Manufactured by Edward F. Caldwell and
Co., New York City
Sterling silver, enamel, wood, ivory, plastic,
and leather
Blotter, H. 15¹⁄₁₆ in. (38.5 cm),
w. 19¹⁄₁₆ in. (48.5 cm)
Penholder, H. 4⅛ in. (10.5 cm),
w. 8⁹⁄₁₆ in. (21.2 cm), D. 3⅝ in. (9.1 cm)
Letter opener, L. 8¾ in. (22.2 cm)
Cigarette box, H. 6¼ in. (15.9 cm),
w. 4¹³⁄₁₆ in. (12.1 cm), D. 4⅜ in. (11.1 cm)
Cigarette box insert, H. 4⅛ in. (10.5 cm),
w. 4 in. (10.2 cm), D. 3½ in. (8.9 cm)
Collection of Albert Nesle, New York City

Many companies specializing in period-
revival decorative arts were stimulated to
experiment with more innovative designs in
the late 1920s. This desk set was handcrafted by several employees of Edward F.
Caldwell and Co., a firm that made fine
quality reproductions in metalwork. The
New York company was founded around
1900 and executed many important commissions, such as metalwork for the interiors of the Waldorf-Astoria Hotel. The firm
dissolved in 1935.[1]

On the cigarette box, ivory panels
depict classical figures in an expertly ren-
dered landscape setting. A tiny animal of
the hunt perches on the cover; inside, an
elaborately pierced silver holder for cigarettes features stylized plant motifs. The
blue enamel used on the ensemble provides a brilliant background for ornament
derived from natural forms. Geometricized
bell flowers on the blotter border and the
cigarette box are adaptations of a traditional neoclassical motif.[2]

1
Information courtesy Albert Nesle, one of
the individuals who worked on this set;
Detroit, *Arts and Crafts in Detroit,* 83.
2
For a contemporary illustration of the cigarette box, see *American Magazine of Art*
24 (April 1932): 273. Source courtesy
W. Scott Braznell.

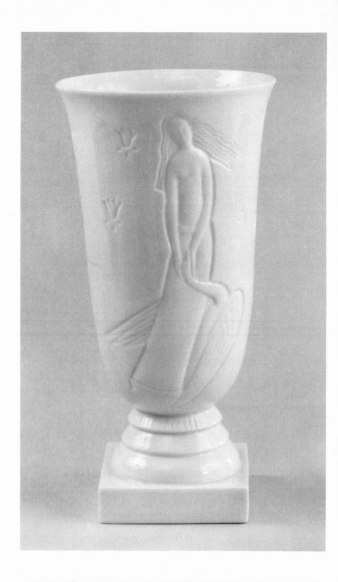

11 Vase
(Leda and the Swan), 1930 to late 1940s
Manufactured by Lenox, Inc., Trenton,
New Jersey
Glazed porcelain
H. 10⅛ in. (26 cm), DIAM. of rim 5⅜ in. (13.1
cm), Base 3½ in. square (8.9 cm)
Transfer printed on underside, "L [inside
laurel wreath]/LENOX/MADE IN U.S.A."
Private Collection

Walter Scott Lenox began producing high-
quality porcelain ware in 1889, and Lenox,
Inc., was soon established as one of the
finest tableware manufacturers in America.[1] Lenox plates and Steuben glassware
were shown at the Metropolitan Museum
in 1926–27 as examples of good design in
useful objects, representing the kinds of
tradition-inspired modern decorative arts
then sanctioned by that institution.[2]
   This vase's pedestal base and flaring
rim resemble a classical urn, although the
traditional form has been elongated. Like
Pablo Picasso and other modern painters,
the designer of this object incorporated a
classical myth into the work. Executed in a
graphic manner with abbreviated lines
outlining the forms, the ornamentation
portrays the myth of Leda and the Swan in
which Zeus takes the shape of a bird in
order to seduce a maiden. This myth was
especially popular during the 1920s;

Henry Varnum Poor constructed a life-sized
fountain depicting Leda and the Swan, and
Donald Deskey designed a rug based on
the same theme.[3]

1
Lenox, Inc., *Lenox China: The Story of
Walter Scott Lenox* (Trenton, N.J., n.d.): 8.
Linda D. Iraca, manager of consumer serv-
ices at Lenox, Inc., states that this design
was manufactured between 1930 and the
late 1940s. Letter to author, 16 March
1983.
2
See The Metropolitan Museum of Art,
*American Industrial Art: Tenth Annual Exhi-
bition of Current Manufactures Designed
and Made in the United States* (New York,
1926), unpaginated.
3
For illustrations, see Henry Varnum Poor, *A
Book of Pottery: From Mud into Immortality* (Englewood Cliffs, N.J.: Prentice-Hall,
1958), 146; and Walter Rendell Storey,
"American Rugs for the Modern Age,"
Creative Art 9 (July 1931): 48.

Fork, Spoon, and Butter Knife
late 1920s to 1931
Designed by Frederick Carder (1863–
1963) for Steuben Division, Corning Glass
Works, Corning, New York
Silver plate and colorless lead glass
Fork, L. 7⅞ in. (20.1 cm)
Spoon, L. 7½ in. (19.1 cm)
Butter knife, L. 4⅛ in. (10.5 cm)
The Rockwell Museum, Corning, New York,
L.83.42.16, .31, .36

Born in England, Frederick Carder began
working in his family's pottery at the age of
fourteen and entered the British glass-pro-
ducing firm Stevens & Williams of Stour-
bridge, Worcestershire, in 1880. In 1903 he
came to this country to observe American
manufacturing processes and became
involved in the establishment of a factory in
Corning, New York.[1] Steuben Glass Works
soon became a leading producer of irides-
cent, handblown glass, often rivaling the
Favrile glass of Louis Comfort Tiffany.[2] Carder's company became a division of Corning Glass Works in 1918.

    Glass-handled flatware was a strik-
ing innovation of this period. Steuben produced these crystal handles for silver plate
companies in Sheffield, England, where the
flatware was assembled. Paul V. Gardner,
a longtime associate of Carder at Steuben,
recalls that the designer originated this
round-handled flatware before 1932.[3]
The colorless glass handles complemented
Steuben's new lines of tableware, such as
"St. Tropez" (cat. 8), introduced in the
early years of the Depression.

    1
Gardner, *Frederick Carder*, 4–7, 21–28.
See also Madigan, *Steuben Glass*, 51–53.
    2
Renwick Gallery, *The Glass of Frederick
Carder* (Washington, D.C.: Smithsonian
Institution, 1972), 1.
    3
Information courtesy Paul V. Gardner. See
Gardner, *Frederick Carder*, 136; ibid., 237
for a line drawing, no. 7478, from the 1932
Steuben catalogue.

13 Bowl
1932
Designed by Walter Dorwin Teague
(1883–1960) for Steuben Division, Corning
Glass Works, Corning, New York
Engraved colorless lead glass
H. 5½ in. (14.1 cm), DIAM. of rim 10 in. (25.4
cm), DIAM. of base 5½ in. (14.1 cm)
Engraved in cursive script on base,
"Steuben"
Anonymous Loan

The profile of this bowl is an adaptation of
the cyma recta molding found in classical
architecture. The foot also has classical
precedents.[1] Walter Dorwin Teague's originality is evident in the engraved circles
that resemble bubbles rising from deep
water. They decrease rather than increase
in size as they near the rim.[2]

    1
Compare the foot of a red-figure Greek
vase, illustrated in John Boardman, *Greek
Art* (New York: Frederick A. Praeger, 1964),
105.
    2
See Gardner, *Frederick Carder,* 322, for a
line drawing of this bowl, no. 7503/T-114,
from the 1932 Steuben catalogue.

14 Tea Service

(Pot, Creamer, Sugar Bowl, and Tray),
1930
Designed and executed by Erik
Magnussen (1884–1961) for August
Dingeldein and Son, New York City
Sterling silver and New Zealand jade
Pot, H. 6³⁄₁₆ in. (15.8 cm)
Creamer, H. 5⅜ in. (13.7 cm)
Sugar bowl, H. 4¹⁵⁄₁₆ in. (9.9 cm)
Tray, L. 22⅝ in. (57.4 cm),
w. 5½ in. (13.9 cm)
Total gross WT. 70 oz. 16 dwt. (2,203 gms)
Marked on undersides of objects,
"EM [conjoined]/ERIK MAGNUSSEN/ADS/
HANAU/GERMANY/STERLING"
Private Collection

Erik Magnussen was born in Denmark and
belonged to the same artistic circle as the
silversmith Georg Jensen (cat. 64). Their
careers are similar in several respects.

Both studied sculpture as young men and
began working with silver in jewelry making. They applied ivory and semiprecious
stones to classically proportioned shapes
and employed restrained floral imagery in
their early work.

Magnussen opened his own workshop in Denmark in 1909. He began working for The Gorham Manufacturing
Company upon arriving in this country in
1925. Because the company was interested in developing modern alternatives to
period-revival silver, he was given a great
deal of artistic freedom. Magnussen's
association with Gorham ended in 1929,[1]
and immediately thereafter he worked for
the firm of August Dingeldein and Son,
which had factories in Germany and a
retail outlet in New York City.

This service was executed by Magnussen at the Dingeldein factory in
Hanau.[2] When it (or an identical service)
was shown in New York City at the Art
Center in 1930 and at the Architectural

League in the next year, several reviewers
compared its unusual form to ancient
Roman and Greek oil lamps.[3] The jade
handles add an oriental exoticism to the
service but have no Chinese or Japanese
precedents. Small curls at the handles'
bases are a subtle abstraction of Magnussen's earlier floral decoration.

The sharp angularity of the service,
however, shows a fundamental transformation of Magnussen's work from his earlier designs (cat. 15). The pot's proportions
and half-circle handle resemble a 1924
teapot by the Bauhaus silversmith Mar-
ianne Brandt,[4] although Magnussen's
forms are both more eccentric and historically referential.

1
Charles H. Carpenter, Jr., *Gorham Silver:
1831–1981* (New York: Dodd, Mead,
1982), 256–58, 264.

2
Erik Magnussen to Louise W. Chase, 12
October 1937, The Brooklyn Museum
Archives, Brooklyn, N.Y., in conjunction
with the exhibition "Contemporary Industrial and Handwrought Silver," 19 November 1937–23 January 1938. Source
courtesy W. Scott Braznell.

3
Walter Rendell Storey, "Fine Art and
Design in New Furnishings," *New York
Times,* 28 September 1930, sec. 5, pp. 14–
15; "They Seem to Agree that Gifts Must
Be Smart," *The Jewelers' Circular* 101
(November 1930): 83. Sources courtesy
W. Scott Braznell.

4
Suggestion courtesy J. Stewart Johnson.
For illustration of Brandt's teapot, see
Arthur Drexler and Greta Daniel, *Introduc-
tion to Twentieth-Century Design from the
Collection of The Museum of Modern Art*
(New York: Museum of Modern Art,
1959), 34.

15 Covered Cup

1926
Designed by Erik Magnussen (1884–1961)
for The Gorham Manufacturing Company,
Providence, Rhode Island
Sterling silver and ivory
H. 8¾ in. (22.2 cm),
DIAM. of rim 6⅝ in. (16.7 cm),
Gross WT. 22 oz. 17 dwt. (711 gms)
Marked on underside of base,
"GORHAM/[Lion, Anchor, G]/STERLING/
EHH/A14006/EM [conjoined]"
Private Collection

In this covered cup, Magnussen maintained the ornamental traditions of his
formative training.[1] The cup displays the
subtly hammered surfaces and the use of
scrolls and beads characteristic of Danish
silver. The reeded ivory stem and the
restrained ornamentation conform to the
taste for neoclassical forms in the 1920s.

1
For a contemporary illustration of Magnus-
sen's cup without the cover, see "Silver in
Modern Designs," *House and Garden* 52
(November 1927): 106. Source courtesy
W. Scott Braznell.

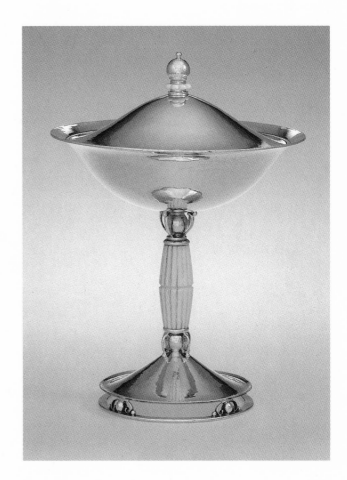

16 Mirror
about 1926
Designed by Paul T. Frankl (1887–1958)
for Frankl Galleries, New York City
Chromium-plated metal, silvered metal,
and glass; tassels not original
H. 36¼ in. (92.1 cm), w. 43 in. (109.2 cm)
Collection of Peter P. Marino,
New York City

Paul Frankl studied architecture and engineering in his native Vienna, as well as in
Paris, Munich, and Berlin. After coming to
the United States in 1914, he applied his
European training to theater design.
Frankl's work reflected not only his Viennese background but also his visit to
Japan early in his career.[1] Many of his
designs were based on oriental models,
although his adaptations were always
more imaginative than literal.

In the late nineteenth century an
enthusiasm for oriental design had a
resurgence in the West and strongly
affected decorative arts throughout the
1920s. In this mirror the tassels and fret-
work at the sides were inspired by oriental
models. The round shape, however,
derives from neoclassical mirrors and was
adopted frequently in the 1920s.[2] Although
Frankl criticized period-revival styles and
espoused a rhetoric of ''no compromise
with tradition,''[3] in practice his modern
designs often relied on historical
precedents.

1
Pierre Migennes, ''Un Artiste décorateur
américain: Paul Th. Frankl,'' *Art et Décora-
tion* 53 (January 1928): 49; *Britannica
Encyclopedia of American Art,* s.v.
''Frankl, Paul T.''
2
For a period illustration of this mirror, see
Clute, *Treatment of Interiors,* 96.
3
Quoted in ''American Modernist Furniture
Inspired by Sky-scraper Architecture,''
Good Furniture Magazine 29 (September
1927): 119.

17 Side Chair
about 1929
Designed by Eugene Schoen (1880–1957)
for Eugene Schoen, Inc., executed by
Schmieg, Hungate and Kotzian,
New York City
Ebonized wood and maple; upholstery not
original
H. 37¼ in. (94.6 cm), w. 20 in. (50.8 cm),
D. 19 in. (48.3 cm)
Museum of Fine Arts, Springfield,
Massachusetts, Gift of Marguerite Kirkham
Hyde. 44.FO1.2a

This side chair originally belonged to a dining room ensemble created for the Fifth
Avenue apartment of Henry Root Stern, a
prominent New York lawyer of the day.[1]
The chair, with its oriental-inspired crest
rail, is similar to a piece illustrated in a
1927 monograph on the work of Josef
Hoffmann.[2] Many modern designers in
Europe and America during the period
made subtle use of eastern prototypes by
simplifying and abstracting oriental forms.
Ebonized and lacquer finishes on furniture
were other aspects of the renewed interest
in decorative arts of the East.
       According to Schoen's design philos-
ophy, a modern style must grow out of
continuity with the past. He wrote in 1928,
"Seriousness, and a thorough knowledge
of what has gone before are the essential
bases of new creations in decoration."[3]

1
Information courtesy Lee Schoen. See R. W.
Sexton, *The Logic of Modern Architecture*
(New York: Architectural Book Publishing
Co., 1929), 113, for period illustration.
       2
For illustration of the Hoffmann chair, see
Daniele Baroni and Antonio D'Auria, *Josef
Hoffmann e la Wiener Werkstätte* (Milan:
Electa, 1981), 174.
       3
Eugene Schoen, "The Design of Modern
Interiors," *Creative Art* 2 (May 1928): xl.

18 Bowl

circa 1930
Designed and executed by
Peter Müller-Munk (1904–1967),
New York City
Sterling silver
H. 2¾ in. (7 cm), W. 7½ in. (19 cm),
D. 5⅛ in. (13 cm),
WT. 10 oz. 8 dwt. (323 gms)
Marked on underside, "P [encircled]/PETER
MULLER-MUNK/HANDWROUGHT/STERLING
SILVER/925/1000"
Yale University Art Gallery, Gift of William
Core Duffy, Mus.B., 1952, Mus.M., 1954,
and Mrs. Duffy. 1980.101

Like Eugene Schoen and Paul Frankl, Peter
Müller-Munk responded to the widespread fascination with oriental decorative
arts. In traditions of the East, American and
European designers found models with
simple well-defined contours and relatively
unornamented surfaces. Despite its small
size, this bowl replicates the monumental
forms of Chinese bronzes, although it
probably does not reproduce any specific
historical example.

19 Bowl

late 1920s to 1931
Designed by Frederick Carder
(1863–1963) for Steuben Division,
Corning Glass Works, Corning, New York
Acid-etched lead glass
H. 6½ in. (16.5 cm), W. 11¾ in. (30 cm),
D. 6¾ in. (17.6 cm)
Etched in relief on bottom edge, "Steuben/
[fleur-de-lis]"
The Chrysler Museum Institute of Glass,
Gift of Walter P. Chrysler, Jr.
GAST 63.14

For this piece Frederick Carder adapted a
traditional Chinese ceramic form, the lotus
bowl.[1] The frosted surface and stylized
rose relate to commercial French glassmaking of the 1920s. The rose motif had
been used earlier by Glasgow and Viennese designers, but contemporaries felt
that the types of stylization used in the
1920s were essentially different from the
aesthetic conventions practiced at the turn
of the century.[2]

1
See Gardner, *Frederick Carder,* 146, for a
pencil drawing of this bowl, no. 8549, from
the 1932 Steuben catalogue.
2
Ackerman, *Wallpaper,* 90–91.

20 Fire Screen
circa 1925
Designed by Wilhelm Hunt Diederich
(1884–1953), New York City
Wrought iron, sheet iron, and steel lathe
H. 30½ in. (77.5 cm), w. 57⅝ in. (146.4 cm)
Collection of Suzanne Vanderwoude,
New York City

Born in Hungary, Hunt Diederich was the grandson of the American painter William Morris Hunt and grandnephew of the architect Richard Morris Hunt. He came from a wealthy background (his father was a large landowner and horse breeder in Hungary). At the age of twenty he studied sculpture at the Pennsylvania Academy of the Fine Arts, and he also received art training in Rome and Paris.[1] Diederich maintained several residences simultane-ously in France, Germany and the United States.

A versatile artist who worked in numerous media, Diederich produced a wide range of objects. Two factors, how-ever, were constant in his art: animal sub-jects, and forms with rhythmic contours and expressive silhouettes. In the cata-logue of his first American exhibition at Kin-gore Galleries, New York, he stated: "As a child of five I embarked upon my artistic career by cutting out silhouettes of animals with a pair of broken-pointed scissors, for I love animals, first, last and always. . . . Animals seem to me truly plastic. They pos-sess such a supple, unspoiled rhythm."[2]

Greyhounds, such as those on this fire screen, were a particular favorite of Diederich's. Perhaps making a visual pun on his own middle name, Diederich con-sistently represented hunting themes by creating animals interlocked in violent motion.[3] In addition to personal symbol-ism, Diederich's work suggests traditional utilitarian metal artifacts such as ornamen-tal fence railings and weathervanes. His ironwork also relates to the metalcrafts of Central American Indians.[4]

1
F. Newlin Price, "Diederich's Adventure in Art," *International Studio* 81 (June 1925): 170.
2
Quoted in Christian Brinton, *Hunt Dieder-ich* (New York: Kingore Galleries, 1920), unpaginated.
3
Suggestion courtesy Diana Diederich Blake.
4
"Indian Craftwork," 216.

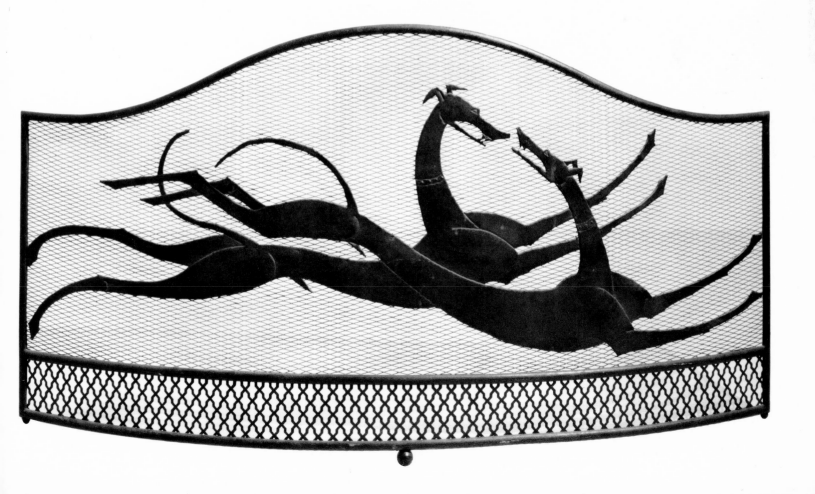

21 Chandelier
circa 1925
Designed by Wilhelm Hunt Diederich
(1884–1953), New York City
Wrought iron
H. 48 in. (121 cm), w. 30 in. (76.2 cm),
D. 30 in. (76.2 cm)
The Newark Museum, 39.180

Like many modern designers of the 1920s,
Hunt Diederich was interested in applying
artistic principles to the production of utilitarian objects. In 1920, Diederich said:

> Art should be useful, should fulfill
> some specific end and purpose in
> our lives and homes. There can be
> as much aesthetic joy in making a
> candlestick or designing the leg of
> a table as in the treatment of the
> nude. . . . Sculpture has been too
> long an affair of marble and
> bronze. It is too remote, too inac-
> cessible. We must do everything
> possible to insure for it a wider,
> more popular acceptance.[1]

Diederich often worked in wrought iron
and sheet metal rather than bronze, the
more traditional material of sculpture. In
New York his designs were executed by
Greenwich Village blacksmiths.[2]

The shape of this chandelier empha-
sizes the inherent qualities of handwrought
metal; its jagged edges suggest the action
of cutting shears. The angular bodies of
the three animals, with their spiky horns
and wildly staring eyes, have some of the
primitive power of totemic art. The motif of
paired rearing ibexes has roots in Mesopotamian art, but animal subjects such as
these are common in the crafts of many
ancient cultures.[3] These creatures are less
tame and saccharine than most of the
exotic animals represented in the decorative arts of this period.

1
Brinton, *Hunt Diederich,* unpaginated.
2
Information courtesy William Diederich.
3
Robert L. Herbert, ''Two Reliefs from Nola,''
Yale University Art Gallery Bulletin 34
(Winter 1974): 12.

Plate

circa 1925
Designed and executed by Wilhelm Hunt
Diederich (1884–1953), New York City
Enamel on copper
H. ¾ in. (1.9 cm), DIAM. 7¾ in. (19.7 cm)
Monogrammed on front, signed "H" on
underside of foot
Collection of Mr. and Mrs. William Hunt
Diederich

Shortly after Hunt Diederich came to America for the first time at the age of sixteen, he spent one of the happiest episodes of his life as a cowboy in Arizona, Wyoming, and New Mexico.[1] The horse on this plate may reflect that formative experience. The color of the object's turquoise enameling as well as the copper material relate to native American crafts of the Southwest.

1
Brinton, *Hunt Diederich,* unpaginated.

23 Bowl

between 1923 and 1927
Designed and executed by Wilhelm Hunt
Diederich (1884–1953), New York City
Lead-glazed earthenware
H. 4¹⁄₁₆ in. (10.3 cm),
DIAM. 15⅜ in. (38.9 cm)
Monogrammed on front
Collection Martin Eidelberg, New York City

Hunt Diederich's interest in ceramics developed around 1923 during a trip to Morocco. He acquired examples of the native pottery and began painting and glazing his own plates and bowls.[1] He won a gold medal for his pottery in 1927 from the Architectural League of New York.[2]

As was typical of his artistic method, Diederich borrowed subjects from his work in other media for his ceramic compositions. This design employs the same rearing ibexes as cat. 21. The lotus palmette below the animals originated in Egypt but also appears on archaic Greek pottery (fig. 2).

1
Information courtesy family of the artist.
2
Who's Who in American Art, 1936–37, s.v. "Diederich, W. Hunt."

24 Vase
1930
Decorated by Lorinda Epply (1874–1951)
for Rookwood Pottery Company,
Cincinnati, Ohio
Glazed semi-porcelain or porcelain
H. 8¼ in. (22 cm),w. 6½ in. (16.5 cm),
D. 6 in. (15 cm)
Signed on underside with Epply
monogram and impressed with RP
fourteen-flame monogram and "xxx/
5203C"
Collection of Ruth and Seymour Geringer

Along with William Hentschel (cat. 25),
Lorinda Epply produced some of the most
individualistic work at the Rookwood Pottery Company during the late 1920s.[1]
Epply attended the Cincinnati Art Academy and studied ceramics at Columbia
University. She worked at Rookwood from
1904 to 1948.[2] Epply and Hentschel represented Rookwood at the Metropolitan
Museum's tenth annual exhibition of industrial art in 1926–27.[3]
    Although the company is now best
known for its ceramics of the arts and
crafts period, Rookwood artists like Epply
produced innovative designs during the
1920s. Given a great deal of artistic freedom, she and other Rookwood ceramists
developed new glazes and novel forms of
ornamentation.[4] The sensuous glaze on
this vase reflects the contemporary concern for lavish color and surface texture.
The schematic fish derive from oriental and
other ancient craft traditions.

1
Herbert Peck, *The Book of Rookwood Pot-
tery* (New York: Crown Publishers, 1968),
109.
    2
Ibid., 144; Virginia Raymond Cummins,
comp., *Rookwood Pottery Potpourri* (Silver
Spring, Md.: Cliff R. Leonard and Duke
Coleman, 1980), 51.
    3
Metropolitan Museum of Art, *American
Industrial Art,* unpaginated.
    4
Peck, *Rookwood Pottery,* 109.

25 Vase
1929
Decorated by William Hentschel
(1882–1962) for Rookwood Pottery
Company, Cincinnati, Ohio
Semi-porcelain or porcelain with blue mat
glaze
H. 16 in. (40.7 cm), DIAM. 7½ in. (19 cm)
Signed on underside with Hentschel
monogram and impressed with RP
fourteen-flame monogram and "xxix/
2984"
Collection of Ruth and Seymour Geringer

William Hentschel attended the Art Students League and studied ceramics, like
Lorinda Epply, at Columbia University. He
was a decorator for Rookwood Pottery
Company from 1907 to 1939.[1]
    In America motifs based on African
themes were less prevalent than in France
during the 1920s. France's extensive
dominions in tropical regions provided
exotic materials (sharkskin, macassar
ebony, ivory, etc.) and formal models for
the country's decorative artists. Some
American ceramists, however, such as Viktor Schreckengost, Russell B. Aitken, and
Hentschel, looked to Africa for design
ideas. In the angular abstract border and
stylized animals and plants on this vase,
Hentschel represents an exotic jungle environment with motifs that are related to
hand-dyed, non-Western textiles.[2]

    1
Cummins, *Rookwood Pottery,* 54–55;
Who's Who in American Art, 1940–41, s.v.
"Hentschel, William."
    2
For an illustration of a pochoir related to
this design, see Kenneth R. Trapp, *Toward
the Modern Style: Rookwood Pottery, the
Later Years: 1915–1950* (New York: Jor-
dan-Volpe Gallery, 1983), 31.

26 Armchair
about 1928
Painted stick willow, cotton and linen
upholstery
H. 37½ in. (95.2 cm), w. 33⅛ in. (84.5 cm),
D. 37½ in. (95.2 cm)
Private Collection

In the New York building boom of the
1920s, many new apartments featured ter-
races and bright sunlit rooms, creating a
new urban context for informal, outdoor
furnishings.[1] Modern designers like Paul
Frankl, Donald Deskey, and Gilbert Rohde
embellished traditional wicker furniture,
popular since the nineteenth century, with
bright paint, bold upholstery, and angular
shapes that often included compartments
to hold reading material and drinking
glasses, such as those on this chair. The
cushions retain their original yellow and
brown fabric, rare for an upholstered
object of this period. Although faded, this
fabric gives a sense of the bold colors and
geometric design motifs common during
the era.[2]

1
Donald Deskey, "Style in Summer Furniture," *Good Furniture and Decoration* 34
(April 1930): 206.
2
The designer and manufacturer of this
piece are unknown.

27 Table Cover

with Backgammon Board Design,
about 1931
Designed by Ilonka Karasz (1896–1981),
executed by Mariska Karasz (1898–1960),
New York City
Crewel on silk grosgrain; cotton velvet
backing
H. 39 in. (99.1 cm), w. 37 in. (94 cm)
Collection of Nathan George Horwitt

Ilonka and Mariska Karasz were sisters
who were born in Budapest, Hungary, and
immigrated to this country in 1913. Ilonka
had attended the Royal School of Arts and
Crafts in her native city.[1] She taught at the
Modern Art School on Washington Square
South, one of the most progressive centers
for art education in New York during the
1910s. Ilonka sold her work at a book-
shop-gallery called The Sunwise Turn,
which presented hand-dyed and embroi-
dered textiles as serious art forms.[2]
According to William Zorach, Ilonka was
one of the most talented and outstanding
personalities in Greenwich Village during
the 1920s.[3] Besides her work in textiles, she
designed ceramics, silver, wallpaper, furniture, book illustrations, and covers for *The
New Yorker.*

   Mariska Karasz concentrated primarily on handworked fabrics. She studied
with Ethel Traphagen at the Cooper Union
Art School in New York.[4] Strongly influenced by Eastern European craft traditions
in her early career, she produced inventive
abstract designs during the 1950s.[5]

   This table cover, with its brightly
colored, stylized floral border surrounding
the black and red backgammon board
design, seems much closer to folk prototypes than does the Karasz wall hanging
(cat. 33). The elaborate needlework is similar in technique to Marguerite Zorach's
work of this period; the intricate chain
stitching adds an active, swirling quality to

the design. Kem Weber chose this textile and cat. 33 to accompany an installation of his designs at the 1931 exhibition of the American Union of Decorative Artists and Craftsmen.[6]

1
American Federation of Arts, *American Art Annual,* 1930, 542; Part of this entry was abstracted from Alice Irma Prather-Moses, comp., "The International Dictionary of Women Workers in the Decorative Arts: A Survey of the Twentieth Century from 1900 to 1975," s.v. "Ilonka Karasz" and "Mariska Karasz" (unpublished manuscript).
2
Roberta K. Tarbell, *Hugo Robus, 1885–1964* (Washington, D.C.: Smithsonian Institution Press for the National Collection of Fine Arts, 1980), 42–43.
3
William Zorach, *Art Is My Life* (Cleveland: World, 1967), 78.
4
"Mariska Karasz," *Interiors* 120 (September 1960): 215.
5
Abstracted from Prather-Moses, "International Dictionary of Women Workers"; see "Reviews and Previews," *Art News* 53 (October 1954): 59.
6
Information courtesy Nathan George Horwitt, a member of AUDAC who was involved with the Weber installation.

8 Wall Hanging

"Syrian Olive Tree,"
between 1919 and 1926
Designed and executed by
Lydia Bush-Brown (b. 1887)
Wax resist-dyed Chinese silk; cotton
backing
H. 81¼ in. (206.5 cm), w. 35½ in. (90 cm)
Monogrammed in lower right corner,
"B [reversed], L, B" above stylized
beech tree
Cooper-Hewitt Museum, The Smithsonian
Institution's National Museum of Design,
Gift of Lydia Bush-Brown. 1974.23.2

Lydia Bush-Brown was a colleague of
Ilonka Karasz, Arthur Crisp, and other
noted textile artists in New York City during
the 1920s.[1] Born in Florence, Italy, to

American parents who were both professional artists, Bush-Brown studied at the Pratt Institute in Brooklyn and then traveled widely, spending a year in Syria.[2] Contact with crafts from the Middle East provided two-dimensional design motifs and thematic inspiration for her textiles.[3] The red and grey borders of this wall hanging represent the mihrab niche that forms the central design of Islamic prayer rugs.[4]

In all of Bush-Brown's work, trees seem to embody cosmic principles, a conception with sources in ancient oriental traditions. The motif under her monogram is an abstract representation of a beech tree. Her "silk murals," as she called them, evoke a kind of delicate, mystical symbolism that did not flourish in the mainstream of decorative arts during the 1930s. The abstract figures, animals, and natural forms, however, that appeared in the work of textile artists such as Bush-Brown, Marguerite and William Zorach, and Arthur Crisp, conform to aesthetic conventions that survived in the architectural mural painting of the next decade.[5]

1
Notebook, "To the Cooper-Hewitt Museum of Design From Lydia Bush-Brown," unpaginated, in the collection of Cooper-Hewitt Museum, New York.
2
Detroit, *Arts and Crafts in Detroit,* 105.
3
"Modernistic Wall Hangings," *Good Furniture Magazine* 31 (August 1928): 108.
4
Compare illustration in Carel J. Du Ry, *The Art of Islam* (New York: Harry N. Abrams, 1970), 183.
5
For a period illustration of this wall hanging, see "Silk Murals for Wall Decorations," *Arts & Decoration* 26 (March 1927): 46. Source courtesy W. Scott Braznell.

MODERN ART

Although the acceptance of decorative arts as equal in importance to painting, sculpture, and architecture is still not universal, in the 1920s the term "modern art" often included the design of useful objects as well as the fine arts.[1] The objects in this section resulted, to a large extent, from a synthetic and broadly inclusive outlook characteristic of the period. Bringing art to every aspect of ordinary existence was the challenge of the day.

To create well-designed and useful objects captured the imagination of painters and sculptors in this country who followed a tradition of interdisciplinary activity established in the nineteenth century. Charles Burchfield designed wallpaper for the M. H. Birge and Sons Company. George Biddle, Thomas Hart Benton, and John Storrs produced rug designs. Charles Sheeler's work included flatware, textile, and glass designs, and the photographer Edward Steichen designed a line of textiles for the Stehli Silk Company.[2] Many designers represented in this exhibition maintained simultaneous careers as painters, sculptors, and architects.

As a result of this interdisciplinary work, decorative designs often reflected major stylistic currents of the 1920s. Especially influential were new forms in architecture (cat. 29), nonobjective painting and sculpture (cats. 30, 31), and the clarity, precision, and machine-tooled elegance of industrial products (cats. 48, 57). Designers also looked back to earlier movements of the twentieth century: fauvism, cubism, and futurism (cats. 34–37, 40–42). Decorative artists tended to adapt these sources eclectically, similar to the use of historical models discussed in the previous section.

Precedents for the interrelationships among the arts of the 1920s existed in the English arts and crafts movement, which proposed a close collaboration between artists, architects, and craftworkers in order to recover the social cohesion of preindustrial civilizations. Participants in later movements such as the Austrian and German Werkbunds, Russian constructivism, Dutch De Stijl, and French purism maintained the ideal of creative collaboration and removed the barriers between the fine and decorative arts. The well-known Bauhaus curriculum erased all distinctions between fine and applied art.[3] Under the influence of Josef Hoffmann, the Wiener Werkstätte also implemented these interdisciplinary concepts. The expertise of Hoffmann and his colleagues ranged from designing buildings to flower vases.

American designers during this period never formulated the kinds of cohesive theories and utopian social programs that their European counterparts did. Many designers born in this country nevertheless learned of vanguard European movements and studied aesthetic innovations in progressive Continental art centers. Ruth Reeves spent most of the 1920s living and working in France,[4] where she studied with Fernand Léger. On returning to the United States, she, like Léger, produced textile designs. "Figures with Still Life" (cat. 34) reflects Reeves's own painting style, derived from a cubist-inspired idiom she developed in Paris. While attending the Slade School of Art in London, Henry Varnum Poor saw the famous 1910 Grafton Gallery exhibition organized by Roger Fry. Paintings by Paul Cézanne, Vincent Van Gogh, Henri Matisse, and Pablo Picasso inspired Poor to study art in Paris.[5] After his return to America, he applied the aesthetics of modern European painting to ceramic forms (cats. 35, 36). Donald Deskey also studied art in Paris, saw the influential Exposition of 1925, and traveled to the Bauhaus in Germany before his return to the United States in 1926.[6] In Europe Deskey was especially impressed by the work of the Dutch De Stijl artists,[7] and one of his early lamps (cat. 30) relates to the movement's diagonal, nonobjective compositions after 1925. The arrival in New York City of European emigrants, such as Joseph Urban, Paul Frankl,

1
The title of an article in *Good Furniture Magazine* 27 (October 1926): 172–74, is a typical example of this tendency. "American Modern Art: Its History and Characteristics" deals with new developments in interior design, not painting and sculpture.

2
See Buffalo Fine Arts Academy/Albright Art Gallery, *Exhibition of Wall Paper, Historical and Contemporary* (Buffalo, N.Y.: 1937), cats. 173–78; "Art Moderne Rugs to the Fore," *Good Furniture Magazine* 31 (September 1928): 140; Constance Rourke, *Charles Sheeler* (New York: Museum of Modern Art, 1939), 53; Kneeland L. Green, "Modern Life, Ordinary Things, Design: Americana Fabrics," *Creative Art* 4 (February 1929): 102.

3
For a description of the Bauhaus curriculum, see Wilk, *Breuer*, 18–19.

4
Harry V. Anderson, "Ruth Reeves," *Design* 37 (March 1936): 24.
5
Detroit, *Arts and Crafts in Detroit,* 81.
6
"Donald Deskey: Pioneer Industrial Designer," undated document in the Donald Deskey Archive, in the Cooper-Hewitt Museum; Roberta Brandes Gratz, "Is Rockefeller Center Losing Its Heart?," *Soho Weekly News,* 12 January 1978, 11; J. Stewart Johnson, "Donald Deskey and American Art Deco," lecture, 22 May 1982, given at the symposium "Design 1925," Fashion Institute of Technology, New York City.

7
Donald Deskey to Linda Steigleder, telephone interview, 30 May 1981. Information courtesy Linda Steigleder.

Figure 3.
Erik Magnussen, Coffee Service,
''The Lights and Shadows of Manhattan,''
manufactured by
The Gorham Manufacturing Company, 1927.
Photograph courtesy Gorham-Textron.

and Wolfgang and Pola Hoffmann from Vienna, Peter Müller-Munk and Walter von Nessen from Berlin, Ilonka and Mariska Karasz from Budapest, and Erik Magnussen from Copenhagen, contributed to the impact of Continental design concepts in this country. Through their work, writings, and participation in exhibitions and organizations, these immigrant designers exerted a great deal of influence.

American and European designers looked to Frank Lloyd Wright as an innovator in establishing a unified relationship between architecture and interior design. His work provided an important conceptual and aesthetic model; Paul Frankl once declared that modern architecture and decoration originated with Wright.[8] Frankl's desk (cat. 29) is similar in concept to Wright's architecturally inspired furniture designs, such as the library table for the Francis W. Little House of 1913.[9] In the years following the 1925 Exposition, advocates of modern style in America, such as Frankl, found few examples of native design innovators to praise. Therefore Wright played an important symbolic role.

Studio potters, glassworkers, and textile artists were inspired by the attitude that their work had expressive possibilities akin to painting, sculpture, and architecture. During this period, they manipulated their media in new ways to create innovative objects. The Viennese ceramist Vally Wieselthier won acclaim at the 1925 Exposition with a humorous and inventive approach to ceramic sculpture (cat. 63). She continued working in this vein after immigrating to America. A major ceramist born in this country, Viktor Schreckengost, studied with Wieselthier's teacher, Michael Polwolny, who founded the ceramic workshop at the Kunstgewerbeschüle in Vienna.[10] Schreckengost absorbed the decorative playfulness of Austrian design (cat. 61). Carl Walters also created ceramic sculptures (cat. 43) influenced by the Austrian spirit. In glassmaking, Maurice Heaton developed art glass with abstract designs (cats. 44, 45) that could also function as tableware.[11] Ilonka and Mariska Karasz produced textiles influenced by modern painting (cat. 33).

Like independent studio craftworkers, manufacturers of decorative arts experimented with applying modern aesthetics to useful objects. The Consolidated Lamp and Glass Company diverged from conventional glass design by creating a pattern related to cubist sculpture. Cat. 41 is probably an example of the company's "Ruba Rombic" line, viewed as frankly "weird" in its own day, yet "so ultra-smart that it is as new as to-morrow's newspaper."[12] While working for The Gorham Manufacturing Company Erik Magnussen departed boldly from tradition in a coffee service called "The Lights and Shadows of Manhattan" (fig. 3). Like the glass vase, this service breaks with conventional form in its cubistic, faceted surfaces. The wallpaper industry developed geometric designs composed of many vibrant colors inspired by modern art (cat. 32). The sage green, fuchsia, and lemon yellow wallpapers of the period contradict the current but mistaken assumption of some "Art Deco" revivalists that the color schemes of the 1920s were exclusively combinations of silver, red, and black.

During the 1950s cultural attitudes toward the interrelationship of the arts in this country changed.[13] Studio craftworkers still looked to painting and sculpture for inspiration, but the rise of totally abstract compositions, formalist art criticism by Clement Greenberg and others, and the skyrocketing prices in New York galleries encouraged an art-for-art's-sake attitude toward the traditional fine arts. The term "modern art" is currently used in a narrower sense than it was in the 1920s, and our culture is far from appreciating contemporary decorative arts with the synthetic vision characteristic of that era.

8
"American Modern Art," 172. See also Dorothy Todd and Raymond Mortimer, *The New Interior Decoration* (New York: Charles Scribner's Sons, 1929), 31.

9
For illustration, see Lisa Phillips, *Shape and Environment: Furniture by American Architects* (New York: Whitney Museum of American Art, 1982), 9.

10
Gordon Forsyth, *20th-Century Ceramics* (London: The Studio, 1936), 124.

11
Information courtesy Maurice Heaton.

12
Shirley Paine, "Shop Windows of Mayfair," *Garden and Home Builder* 47 (July 1928): 510. Source courtesy W. Scott Braznell.

13
One example of this trend was the discontinuation in the 1950s of museum-sponsored design exhibitions. See Horn, "MOMA's 'Good Design' Programs," *passim*.

29 Desk
about 1930
Designed by Paul T. Frankl (1887–1958) for
Frankl Galleries, New York City
Ebonized wood and zebrawood
H. 46½ in. (118.2 cm), w. 52 in. (132 cm),
D. 22½ in. (57.2 cm)
Labeled on back with metal plate,
"SKYSCRAPER FURNITURE / 2313"
The George Walter Vincent Smith Art
Museum, Springfield, Massachusetts,
17.78.05

When Paul Frankl's name first appeared in
the 1916–17 Manhattan city directory, his
profession was listed as architect.[1]
Although primarily a decorator, Frankl
relied on his architectural training in furniture design. Unlike cat. 46, this desk does
not literally represent New York skyscrapers but embodies the current interest
of architects in horizontal relationships of
form. Frank Lloyd Wright had opened up
the boxy shapes of traditional buildings,
and International Style architects, such as
Walter Gropius and Le Corbusier, created
buildings consisting of rhythmically discon-
nected and intersecting planes. Frankl's
desk embodies a similar sense of free-
floating planes, but Wright, Le Corbusier,
and Gropius would not have employed the
expensive wood used here. In its lavish
materials the object relates to the work of
French furniture designers such as Djo-
Bourgeois and Jean-Jacques Adnet.[2]

1
Polk and Co.'s, *New York Directory,*
1916–17, s.v. "Frankl, Paul T."
2
Compare illustrations of these two French
designers' work in Holme and Wainwright,
Decorative Art 1929, 80, 133. For period
illustration, see Paul T. Frankl, *Form and Re-
form* (New York: Harper and Brothers,
1930), 136.

30 Table Lamp
1926–27
Designed by Donald Deskey (b. 1894) for
Deskey–Vollmer, Inc., New York City
Glass, chromium-plated brass, and wood
H. 11 in. (27.9 cm), w. 8⅝ in. (22 cm),
D. 5⅜ in. (14 cm)
Paper label on underside of base,
"Deskey–Vollmer"
The Metropolitan Museum of Art, Gift of
Theodore R. Gamble, Jr., in honor of Mrs.
Robert Gamble, 1982. 1982.33

Donald Deskey studied architecture at the
University of California, Berkeley, and
painting at the Art Students League of New
York City and the School of the Art Institute
of Chicago.[1] Upon moving to New York
after World War I, he worked briefly in
advertising but soon began pursuing a
career as a painter. He made two trips to
France in the early 1920s and was enrolled
at the Ecole de la Grande Chaumière in
Paris. Deskey returned to New York City in
1926 and began working as an interior
designer. His first commissions were modern display windows for the Franklin Simon
and Saks Fifth Avenue department stores,
which incorporated backdrops made of
industrial materials with the high-fashion
merchandise. He also produced hand-
painted screens for Paul Frankl's gallery
and designed apartment interiors for
Adam Gimbel and other prominent New
Yorkers. In 1927 Deskey became associated with Phillip Vollmer and established
Deskey-Vollmer, Inc., a company that
lasted until the early 1930s.[2] Deskey continued to receive important commissions,
such as the design of the interiors of Radio
City Music Hall.

    Like French designers such as Jean
Puiforcat (cat. 65), Deskey was influenced
by avant-garde painting and sculpture.
The diagonal design on the frosted glass
of this Deskey-Vollmer lamp relates to nonobjective compositions of the 1920s, especially the post-1925 work of the Dutch De
Stijl artist Theo van Doesburg. Deskey may
have had more immediate models in the
contemporary designs of French glass-
makers.[3] The lamp's fluted base also
reveals the same influence of neoclassical
tradition as in modern French and Austrian
design.

1
Resume, 1938, "Biography of Donald
Deskey" file, Donald Deskey Archive,
Cooper-Hewitt Museum.
    2
Donald Deskey to author, conversation,
27 April 1983.
    3
Compare a design by Maurius-Ernest
Sabino in Holme and Wainwright, *Decora-
tive Art 1929,* 183. For a period illustration
of the lamp, see *House and Garden* 55
(March 1929): 101.

1 Vase
1930
Designed and executed by Richard O.
Hummel (about 1899–about 1976) for
Cowan Pottery Studio, Rocky River, Ohio
Lead-glazed earthenware
H. 8 in. (20.3 cm),
DIAM. of rim 4½ in. (11.5 cm)
Signed on underside "ROH/1930,"
impressed "COWAN" as the upper part of a
circle with "RG" inside
The Brooklyn Museum, H. Randolph Lever
Fund. 72.40.25

R. Guy Cowan first opened his studio in
1912, and such well-known ceramic artists
as Russell B. Aitken, Thelma Frazier, Arthur
E. Baggs, Waylande Gregory, and Viktor
Schreckengost were affiliated with the
company. Cowan produced both commercial and art pottery, but in 1929 the market
for limited-edition and unique ceramic
pieces began to diminish. In December
1930 the company went into receivership
but remained open for one more year to
use up materials in stock. Without commercial pressures the Cowan artists experimented freely, and some of the studio's
most creative output dates from this
period.[1] Although based in Ohio, the company was involved in the promotion of
modern design in New York City. Cowan

was represented at the Metropolitan
Museum's annual exhibitions of industrial
art and also at the 1927 and 1928 design
exhibitions held at Macy's department
store.

Little is known of Richard O. Hummel's life. In 1913 he began working at
Cowan, and he later became the studio
chemist. He also glazed the work of other
ceramists.[2] In his spare time, he threw his
own innovative pieces. His work was
shown at the Metropolitan Museum of Art
and the Cleveland Museum of Art, but
ironically Hummel never considered himself a ceramic artist.[3] The circular design
on this vase employs the geometric simplification of nonobjective art during the
1920s. The contrast of black background
and white circles also relates to the work of
French ceramists, such as René Buthaud.

1
Rocky River Public Library, *Cowan Pottery
Museum* (Rocky River, Ohio, 1978), 4–6.
2
Information courtesy George W. Scherma,
director of the Rocky River Public Library.
3
Richard Hummel to Frances Hirst, 9
December 1969; letter courtesy George W.
Scherma.

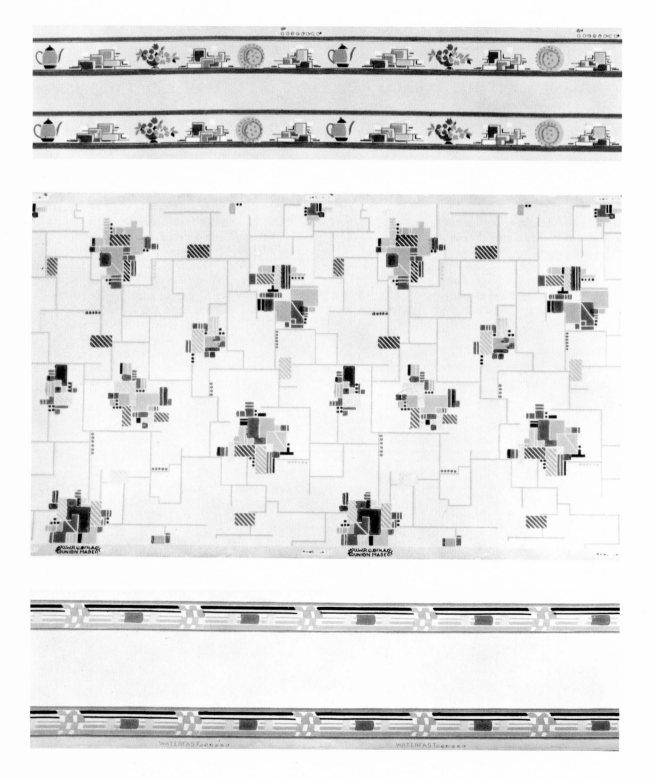

Wallpaper and Two Borders
about 1929 to 1932
Manufactured by the M. H. Birge and Sons
Company, Buffalo, New York
Colored and silver inks on paper
Wallpaper, w. 17³⁄₁₆ in. (44.2 cm),
Repeat 15¹¹⁄₁₆ in. (39.8 cm)
Border with kitchen design,
w. 2 in. (3.1 cm), Repeat 16 in. (40.6 cm)
Border with abstract design,
w. 1⅝ in. (4.2 cm), Repeat 6¼ in. (16 cm)
Printed on selvage of abstract border,
"BIRGE—MADE IN USA/CONFORMS TO
GOVERNMENT STANDARDS/WATERFAST"
Printed on selvage of wallpaper and
abstract border, "U.W.P.C. OF N.A./UNION
MADE," surrounded by the letters "A," "F,"
"O," and "L" within semicircles
Collection of Suzanne Lipschutz,
Secondhand Rose, New York City

In 1930 the M. H. Birge and Sons Company, one of the oldest wallpaper manufacturers in America, had been in business for almost a century. Most of their designs in the 1920s were conservative period reproductions, but in the late 1920s the company introduced new lines. The company most likely responded to the growing popularity of imported European papers, such as the "Salubra" patterns, designed by members of the Wiener Werkstätte and sold through Frederick Blank and Company, Inc., in New York.[1] The Birge Company participated in the Metropolitan Museum of Art's tenth annual industrial art exhibition in 1926.

The designer of this wallpaper is not known, but the asymmetrical silvered composition with bright accents of color is similar in feeling to the sophisticated silk-screened catalogue covers and posters of the era. The abstract border shows the influence of Wiener Werkstätte design, while the border with the kitchen motif, depicting homey blue teapots and yellow plates, adapts the modern idiom to conservative American taste. The development of waterproof and colorfast papers in the late 1920s contributed to the increasing use of bold colors in the wallpaper industry.[2]

1
See Buffalo Fine Arts Academy, *Exhibition of Wallpaper*, cats. 210–15. See also Sexton, *Modern Architecture*, 116.
2
Frank W. Copley and W. H. Glover, "The Birge Story," *Niagara Frontier* 6 (Spring 1959): 10.

33 Wall Hanging
about 1931
Designed by Ilonka Karasz (1896–1981),
executed by Mariska Karasz (1898–1960),
New York City
Crewel on canvas in overlaid and chain
stitches
H. 24½ in. (62.2 cm), w. 47½ in. (120.7 cm)
Collection Richard A. Lukins

Mariska Karasz executed this wall hanging in traditional embroidery stitches, employing heavy crewels in shades of pink, blue, green, and yellow. The figures and landscape, designed by her sister Ilonka, were originally much brighter. Conceived in a consciously naïve mode, the work relates to fauve and German expressionist painting, particularly arcadian scenes by Henri Matisse. Female figures surrounded by graceful animals (usually some kind of deer) were common motifs in the decorative arts of the period. This work, along with cat. 27, was displayed in the 1931 American Union of Decorative Artists and Craftsmen exhibition.

34 Wall Hanging

"Figures with Still Life" pattern, 1930
Designed by Ruth Reeves (1892–1966)
for W. & J. Sloane, New York City
Block-printed cotton velvet
H. 91⅜ in. (233 cm), w. 46 in. (116.8 cm)
Printed signature at lower left,
"RUTH REEVES"
Collection JHS, New York City

Ruth Reeves attended the Pratt Institute in Brooklyn from 1910 to 1911, and in 1913 she won a scholarship to study at the Art Students League in New York. She was in Paris from 1920 to 1927 and studied with Fernand Léger at the Académie Moderne.[1] Before going to France, she lived in a room above Maurice Heaton's family in Greenwich Village. Heaton and Reeves became friends and maintained contact after both settled in Rockland County, New York, a country retreat for many Manhattan artists, writers, and theater professionals in the early twentieth century.[2]

Reeves designed handblocked textiles after returning to the United States in the late 1920s. In 1930, W. & J. Sloane commissioned her to design modern fabrics for a country house. For this textile—executed in warm brown tones on velvet—Reeves was inspired by the subject matter, style, and scale of cubist paintings by Pablo Picasso and Léger. Part of the Sloane series, "Figures with Still Life" was included in a one-woman exhibition at the Art Center, New York, featuring Reeves's paintings, drawings, and textile designs. One reviewer wrote:

> Shown together, these paintings and finished textiles present a clear view of the method and manner in which Miss Reeves has so successfully adapted work in one medium to such excellent effect in another. Also, the display shows the close relationship between the fine and applied arts. . . . This collection proves again that . . . fine arts are coming to have a more and more important influence in industry.[3]

1
Millia Davenport to author, conversation, 22 January 1983, and from Ruth Reeves's resume, courtesy Duny Katzman. Some of the information in this entry and subsequent entries on Reeves is extracted from Prather-Moses, "International Dictionary of Women Workers," s.v. "Ruth Reeves."
2
Information courtesy Maurice Heaton; Tarbell, *Hugo Robus,* 44–45.
3
Blanche Naylor, "Textiles Derived from Paintings," *Design* 33 (February 1932): 214.

35 Plate
between 1921 and 1924
Designed and executed by Henry Varnum
Poor (1888–1971), New City, New York
Earthenware covered on front with white
slip under a lead glaze
DIAM. 8 in. (20.3 cm)
Signed on front, "HVP," and impressed
twice on underside with Crowhouse mark
Collection Martin Eidelberg, New York City

Henry Varnum Poor studied painting at
Stanford University, at the Slade School of
Art in London (1910), and the Académie
Julien in Paris (1911). He taught art at
Stanford after returning to America and
settled in New York City following World
War I.[1] Unable to subsist through the sale
of his paintings, he began producing
ceramics as a means of making a living.
Poor spent twelve hours a day teaching
himself the craft of pottery making and
completely ceased painting for the decade
of the 1920s. He adopted the Persian technique of painting or etching a design on
damp slip before applying the glaze to a
ceramic piece.[2]

Poor's earliest works were marked
with an impressed symbol representing
Crowhouse, the rustic studio he built in a
secluded area of Rockland County, New
York. He eventually signed and sold his
pieces through Manhattan art galleries but
always intended his ceramics to be used.[3]
A warped plate did not matter to Poor, who
aimed for spontaneity in both ceramic form
and decoration. Above all he sought to
avoid "the sterile preciousness of the 'artist
potter'."[4]

Although this plate and cat. 36 were
produced before 1925, they are representative of Poor's ceramic output throughout
the 1920s. In this work, striking green and
brown color divisions on the woman's face
resemble Henri Matisse's famous portrait
of his wife, now in the State Museum of Art,
Copenhagen. The harsh shadows and
angularity of the composition, however,
seem more closely related to the work of
the German expressionist Ernst Ludwig
Kirchner.

1
Detroit, *Arts and Crafts in Detroit,* 81.
2
Poor, *Book of Pottery,* 7, 42–43.
3
Walter Gutman, "Four Potters," *The Arts* 14
(September 1928): 154–55.
4
Poor, *Book of Pottery,* 43.

36 Plate
between 1921 and 1924
Designed and executed by Henry Varnum
Poor (1888–1971), New City, New York
Earthenware covered on front with white
slip under a lead glaze
DIAM. 8¼ in. (21.1 cm)
Signed on front, "HVP," and impressed
twice on underside with Crowhouse mark
Collection JHS, New York City

In technique the painting on this yellow
and blue plate resembles washes of water-
color, whereas the juxtaposition of the floral patterns against the bowl of fruit is a
compositional device borrowed from synthetic cubist works, especially the still lifes
of Georges Braque and Juan Gris. Henry
Varnum Poor often depicted the traditional
genres of painting (portraits, still life,
nudes, and landscapes) in ceramic decoration, enclosed in freely painted abstract
border designs.

37 Vase

1930

Decorated by Jens Jacob Herring Krog
Jensen (1895–1978) for Rookwood Pottery
Company, Cincinnati, Ohio
Semi-porcelain or porcelain with wax mat
glaze
H. 9⅜ in. (23.8 cm), DIAM. 8½ in. (20.4 cm)
Signed on underside with Jensen
monogram; impressed with RP fourteen-
flame monogram, "XXX/5204B," and with
printed Fiftieth Anniversary kiln mark
Collection of Ruth and Seymour Geringer

Jens Jensen was a Danish artist who studied at the Ryslinge and Askov Academy in
Jutland and immigrated to the United
States in 1927. He worked for the Rookwood Pottery Company from 1928 to
1948.[1]

  Jensen's vase, with its flattened,
rose-colored flowers, relates to a decorative cubist idiom practiced by French painters and decorative artists, such as Marie
Laurencin, during the 1920s. Rookwood
artists a few decades earlier had begun
treating the ceramic surface as if it were a
painter's canvas, creating misty landscapes evocative of impressionist paintings. During the 1920s Jensen, William
Hentschel, and Wilhelmine Rehm continued to use contemporary paintings as
sources of inspiration. These three artists
were Rookwood's representatives at the
Metropolitan Museum's 1931 exhibition of
industrial art.[2]

  1
Peck, *Rookwood Pottery,* 145; Cummins,
Rookwood Pottery, 67.
  2
The Metropolitan Museum of Art, *Twelfth
Exhibition of Contemporary American
Industrial Art* (New York, 1931),
unpaginated.

38 Vase

1931

Decorated by Jens Jacob Herring Krog
Jensen (1895–1978) for Rookwood Pottery
Company, Cincinnati, Ohio
Semi-porcelain or porcelain with clear,
high-gloss glaze
H. 9½ in. (24.1 cm), DIAM. 4½ in. (11.5 cm)
Signed on underside with Jensen
monogram; impressed with RP fourteen-
flame monogram and "XXXI/1121C/[six
wedge-shaped marks]"
Collection of Rosalie M. Berberian

In the 1920s Rookwood artists introduced
new glazes that produced indistinct, floating outlines and curdled areas of color.[1]
Jens Jensen worked frequently with these
glazes and often placed lithe figures
against deeply saturated blue backgrounds. The undulating nudes on this
vase appear submerged in an ambiguous
underwater world. Well versed in modern
painting styles, Jensen made skillful, if
eclectic, adaptations based on the work of
several contemporary artists. The elongated figures in this piece relate to images
of women painted by Amedeo Modigliani.

  1
Peck, *Rookwood Pottery,* 108.

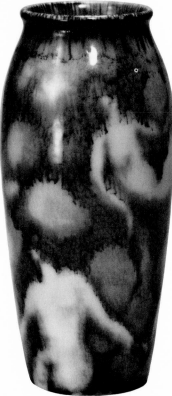

39 Bowl

1930
Decorated by Wilhelmine Rehm
(1899–1967) for Rookwood Pottery
Company, Cincinnati, Ohio
Semi-porcelain or porcelain with wax mat
glaze
H. 3⅛ in. (8 cm),
DIAM. of rim 8⅛ in. (20.6 cm)
Signed on underside with Rehm
monogram; impressed with RP fourteen-
flame monogram, "XXX/2253C"; paper
label printed with Rookwood monogram
and "Remove/only when sold," inscribed
"Wax Mat/No. 444/2253C/$20"
The Brooklyn Museum, H. Randolph Lever
Fund. 72.40.16

Wilhelmine Rehm was a graduate of Smith
College, the University of Cincinnati, and
the Cincinnati Art Academy. She came to
the Rookwood Pottery in 1927 and stayed
until 1935. She then taught public school
and worked as a glass designer until 1943
when she returned to Rookwood. Rehm
was one of the Rookwood ceramists represented at the Metropolitan Museum's 1931
exhibition of industrial art.[1]

   Most of a decorator's work at Rookwood consisted of painting precast pieces,
but Rehm also worked as a modeler. The
wax mat glaze on this bowl, which is docu-
mented by a paper label from the factory,
contributes to the tactile quality of the surface; the naturalistic shapes are submerged in the abstract pattern of the
design.

1
Cummins, *Rookwood Pottery,* 69; Metropolitan Museum of Art, *Twelfth Exhibition
of Industrial Art,* unpaginated.

40 Chess Piece

circa 1925
Designed by Wilhelm Hunt Diederich
(1884–1953), executed by M. Noack,
Berlin, Germany
Bronze
H. 3¼ in. (8.2 cm), w. 1½ in. (3.9 cm),
D. 2⅜ in. (6 cm)
Stamped on back side, "M. NOACK/
BERLIN/FRIEDENAU"
Collection of Diana Diederich Blake,
Baltimore, Maryland

Of all the designers represented in this
exhibition, Hunt Diederich most energeti-
cally displayed the persona of an aristocratic bohemian. In 1913 he received
praise for a sculpture of three greyhounds
exhibited at the Paris Salon d'Automne.
Three years later he erected the piece on
an unused pedestal in Central Park. Offi-
cials considered the incident a prank, and
the piece was removed. Diederich's work
was later permanently integrated into the
architecture of the Central Park Zoo.[1]

In his own day Diederich's art was
called "both sophisticated and elemental,
both patrician and primitive."[2] This chess
piece, originally part of a full set, displays
the abstract faceting of cubist and German
expressionist sculpture.

1
Obituary, *New York Times,* 16 May 1953,
p. 19; Price, "Diederich's Adventure in
Art," 172. The weathervanes that top many
of the buildings in the Central Park Zoo are
reproduced from Diederich's original
designs. Information courtesy R. Craig
Miller.
2
Brinton, *Hunt Diederich,* unpaginated.

41 Vase

probably "Ruba Rombic" pattern,
about 1928
Probably manufactured by
Consolidated Lamp and Glass Company,
Coraopolis, Pennsylvania
Mat gray non-lead glass
H. 6¼ in. (15.9 cm), w. 4⅞ in. (12.4 cm),
D. 4½ in. (11.4 cm)
Private Collection

Although this vase is unmarked, its shape
relates closely to the "Ruba Rombic" pattern illustrated in a 1928 advertisement.
Regarding the pattern's arcane name, the
advertisement explains, "Rubaiy (meaning
epic or poem) Rombic (meaning irregular
in shape)." Of the glassware's unusual
form, it states:

> In our architecture today we find
> the curve supplanted by straight
> lines—because the modern archi-
> tect has learned how to support
> masonry without the aid of the old
> arches, trusses and pilasters that
> were once necessary. And when
> you come to think of it, there is no
> real reason why a vase should be
> spherical instead of angular, is
> there?[1]

This "anything goes" attitude motivated
some of the more wildly inventive decorative arts produced at the end of the 1920s.
During the more sober 1930s, experiments
in disjunctive forms, such as this vase, were
sharply criticized and blamed for giving
modern design a bad name.[2]

1
Reproduced in Hazel Marie Weatherman,
Colored Glass of the Depression Era 2
(Ozark, Mo.: Weatherman Glassbooks,
1974), 48; for another period illustration,
see Paine, "Shop Windows," 510.
2
See, for example, Donald Deskey, "The
Rise of American Architecture and Design,"
The London Studio 5 (April 1933): 268. In
the 1930s objects like this vase had come
to be called "modernistic," a generally
pejorative term by that time.

Bookends
about 1927
Designed by Russel Wright (1904–1976)
New York City
Nickel-plated metal
H. 5⅜ in. (12.3 cm), W. 6¼ in. (15.8 cm),
D. 2¹⁵/₁₆ in. (7.9 cm)
Yale University Art Gallery, Gift of
J. Marshall and Thomas M. Osborn in
memory of Mr. and Mrs. James M.
Osborn. 1977.40.14A & B

Russel Wright briefly studied painting with
Frank Duveneck at the Cincinnati Art
Academy, took classes at the Art Students
League in 1920, and was enrolled in the
Columbia University School of Architecture
in 1923.[1] He began his career in 1924 as a
theater designer, but became involved in
the decorative arts in 1927 when he began
casting miniature versions of his papier-
mâché stage props, such as these horses,
into metal.[2] In their bulging, muscular legs
and stylized manes, these tiny faceless
horses display futurist conventions for representing motion. Extremely heavy for their
size, these horses were used as bookends,
but a journal of the time sarcastically
called them "useless objects d'art."[3]

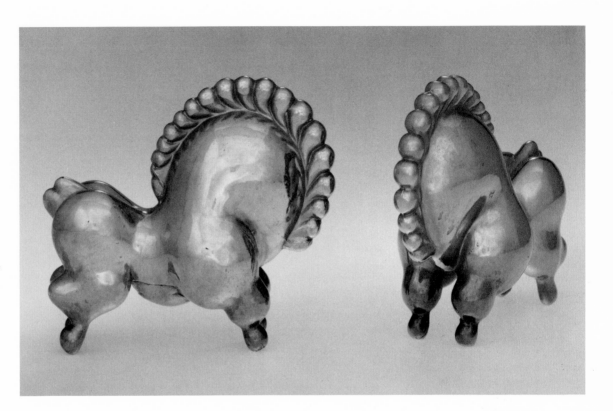

        1
Who's Who in American Art, 1973, s.v.
"Wright, Russel"; "Russel Wright,"
undated summary of Wright's career in the
Russel Wright Archive, George Arents
Research Library, Syracuse University,
Syracuse, N.Y.
        2
Meikle, *Twentieth Century Limited,* 42.
        3
Unidentified clipping, Gilbert Rohde scrap-
book, collection of Lee Rohde. Access
courtesy David Hanks and Derek Oster-
gard. For a period illustration, see *Vogue*
74 (3 August 1929): 52. Source courtesy
W. Scott Braznell.

43 Figure of a Pig

1930
Designed and executed by Carl Walters
(1883–1955), Woodstock, New York
Lead-glazed earthenware
H. 8⅛ in. (20.6 cm), L. 17¾ in. (45.1 cm),
W. 5¾ in. (14.6 cm)
Incised on underside, "[circle in square]/
WALTERS/19 30/[horse's head in profile
to left]"
Collection JHS, New York City

Carl Walters studied at the Minneapolis
School of Art from 1905 to 1907, and continued his education as a painter with Robert Henri at the Chase School in New York
City from 1908 to 1911. In 1919 he began
making ceramics and set up his first workshop in Cornish, New Hampshire, but
moved to Woodstock, New York, in the
next year.[1]

    Walters's first ceramic forms were
candlesticks, bowls, vases, and plates
ornamented with calligraphic designs
related to Persian pottery. He began producing whimsical ceramic animals by
assembling hollow cylinders of clay.[2] This
pig, with pointed ears, spurs and snout,
curly tail, and oversized eyes, has a comic
and mischievous persona similar to Wiener
Werkstätte figurines, yet it lacks their
slightly sinister quality. The purple spots on
the body, which do not mimic the actual
coloring of a pig, can be appreciated as a
purely abstract pattern of colors and
shapes.

    1
Clark, *Century of Ceramics*, 338.
    2
"Carl Walters—Sculptor of Ceramics,"
Index of Twentieth-Century Artists 3 (June
1936): 305.

Salad Bowl

about 1930
Designed and executed by
Maurice Heaton (b. 1900),
Valley Cottage, New York
Colorless glass with white enamel glaze
DIAM. 14 in. (35.7 cm)
Signed on underside, "M.H."
Alan Moss Studios, New York City

After coming to New York City from his
native Switzerland at the age of ten, Maurice Heaton attended the Ethical Culture
School from 1915 to 1919. This institution
advocated a progressive approach to
education that emphasized service to others and skepticism about received knowledge. From 1920 to 1921 he studied
engineering at the Stevens Institute of
Technology in Hoboken, New Jersey.[1]
A long apprenticeship under his father,
Clement Heaton—a noted English stained-
glass artist who worked in Switzerland
before coming to the United States—introduced Maurice to glassmaking techniques.
The son's willingness to question traditional methods led him to new techniques
for producing innovative glass.[2]

Heaton began making modern
designs in the late 1920s, experimenting
with white, translucent enamel glazes on
handcut sheets of bubbly glass. He created the enamel spirals, such as those on
this bowl, while turning the glass on a
device similar to a potter's wheel. His work
impressed a contemporary reviewer as
"entirely different from any of the familiar
types of craftsmanship in glass."[3]

1
Who's Who in American Art, 1980, s.v.
"Heaton, Maurice."
2
Information courtesy Maurice Heaton.
3
Eugene Clute, "Craftsmanship in Deco-
rated Glass," *Architecture* 64 (July 1931):
11. For a period illustration of glass similar
to this design and cat. 45, see Blanche
Naylor, "National Alliance of Art and
Industry Shows New Design Trends,"
Design 36 (May 1934): 4.

45 Plate

about 1930
Designed and executed by
Maurice Heaton (b. 1900),
Valley Cottage, New York
Colorless glass with green enamel glaze
DIAM. 9⅞ in. (25.1 cm)
Signed on underside, "M.H."
The Metropolitan Museum of Art,
Gift of Maurice Heaton, 1979.
1979.194.

Maurice Heaton's designs attracted the
attention of several members of the Architectural League of New York, and through
these contacts his work became well
known. Eugene Schoen and Rena Rosenthal sold his glass at their galleries.[1]
Schoen also employed Heaton to design
and execute large glass murals in several
interiors. The most ambitious of these was
*The Flight of Amelia Earhart Across the
Atlantic* for the RKO theater in Rockefeller
Center.[2] Unfortunately the theater and
mural were destroyed in 1954.

From the beginning of his career,
Heaton was interested in producing art
glass at an affordable price. For the geometric pattern on this plate, he sprinkled
powdered green glaze over a stencil
before firing the object.[3] Heaton still pro-
duces handcrafted glass today at his studio in Rockland County, using many of the
techniques and designs he developed at
the beginning of his career.

1
Information courtesy Maurice Heaton.
2
See "An Illuminated Glass Mural," *Architecture* 66 (December 1932): 351.
3
Eleanor Bitterman, "Heaton's Wizardry
with Glass," *Craft Horizons* 14
(June 1954): 13.

URBAN LIFE

Together with traditional models and aesthetic developments in the other arts, the modern urban environment provided a rich source for new design ideas in the late 1920s. During this era modern designers began looking to technological developments, such as airplane flight, talking pictures, electric lights, and radio communication, for design concepts appropriate to modern times (cats. 59, 60). Particularly in New York City, both urban architecture and new patterns in domestic and social life inspired innovations in the decorative arts.

No city contained more inspiring urban images than New York, and much of its unique character derived from its soaring architecture. Numerous American painters and sculptors, such as Georgia O'Keeffe, Joseph Stella, John Marin, Charles Sheeler, and John Storrs, portrayed Manhattan skyscrapers in some of their most powerful works. New York architecture also served those designers, like Paul Frankl (cat. 46), Ilonka Karasz (fig. 4), and Ruth Reeves (cat. 47), who looked to it as an expression of contemporary American life and values.

Part of the fascination with New York's architecture in the 1920s was due to its rapidly changing character. An economic boom provided funds for ambitious, multimillion-dollar architectural projects. Since the late nineteenth century, skyscrapers by Louis Sullivan and other Chicago and New York architects had captured the popular imagination. When the Woolworth Building was erected in 1913 as the world's tallest office building, it soon became a new symbol of America's commercial power. Crowned with Gothic spires, the building was called a "cathedral of commerce." Other skyscrapers erected in the 1910s and 1920s displayed classical ornamentation on their towering facades.

In 1922 *The Chicago Tribune* held an international competition for the design of a new office building—an event that altered skyscraper design. John Mead Howells and Raymond Hood won the competition with an ornate Gothic tower, but the second-place entry submitted by the Finnish architect Eliel Saarinen received much attention. Eloquently praised by Louis Sullivan, the design integrated restrained detailing with simple rectangular masses diminishing in size toward the top. Saarinen's design became a frequently used model for later skyscrapers; Hood himself, upon receiving the commission for the American Radiator Building in New York City (1924), prepared an elevation close to Saarinen's entry.[1]

New building regulations were also transforming the skyline of Manhattan. Concerned with maintaining enough light and fresh air for surrounding buildings and pedestrians, the city instituted strict codes in 1916 that required roof setbacks after a certain height; the higher the building, the more setbacks were prescribed.[2] These requirements inhibited the design of skyscrapers as continuous vertical shafts with Gothic spires or classical cornices.[3] The necessity of erecting buildings with irregular profiles suggested non-Western historical precedents. Many New York skyscrapers in the late 1920s displayed the stepped-back silhouettes of Aztec, Mayan, and ancient Mesopotamian monumental architecture. Two of the best examples of setback skyscrapers still stand in New York: Ely Jacques Kahn's office building at Two Park Avenue (1927) and the Chanin Building (1929) on Lexington Avenue.

As skyscrapers grew taller and more numerous in the 1920s, few observers, except Lewis Mumford and a handful of other prescient critics, were concerned about what this unrestrained expansion of the New York skyline would contribute to congestion and pollution in an already overcrowded metropolis.[4] Most critics saw Manhattan's rapidly rising skyline as an inspirational symbol of American achievement.

1
Albert Christ-Janer, *Eliel Saarinen* (Chicago: University of Chicago Press, 1948), 55–58; Robert A. M. Stern with Thomas P. Catalano, *Raymond M. Hood* (New York: Rizzoli, 1982), 10–11.

2
Dan Klein, "The Chanin Building, New York," *The Connoisseur* 186 (July 1974): 163.

3
Carol Herselle Krinsky, *Rockefeller Center* (New York: Oxford University Press, 1978), 18.

4
See Lewis Mumford, "Art in the Machine Age," *The Saturday Review of Literature,* 8 September 1928, pp. 102–103.

Figure 4.
Ilonka Karasz, Studio Apartment, about 1929.
Reproduced from C. Geoffrey Holme
and Shirley B. Wainwright, eds.,
Decorative Art 1929: Creative Art Yearbook
(New York: Albert and Charles Boni, 1929), 147.
Permission courtesy Readex Microprints, Inc.

An architect of the period, R. W. Sexton, wrote in 1929:

> Can we not see in this emphasis of vertical lines certain traits of American life of this day and
> generation? May we not think that these prominent vertical lines reflect our eagerness to attain
> that which has been considered heretofore out of our reach? Do they not interpret our striving to
> solve unknown mysteries? Do not these vertical lines interpret . . . our tendency towards "speed-
> ing up," our nervous restlessness? And the simple forms and masses which they outline:—Are they
> not suggestive of our democratic spirit?[5]

5
Sexton, *Modern Architecture,* 92.

The skyscraper had been repeatedly identified with the American spirit since the late nineteenth century;
like Frank Lloyd Wright's architecture, it was one of the few original American contributions to modern
design that contemporaries in the 1920s pointed to with pride.

Skyscraper imagery began to transform even the domestic interior by the late 1920s. Although Paul
Frankl wrote in 1928, "The home is a place that is still sacred and will not tolerate too many experiments or
novelties,"[6] a changing urban architecture had by this time convinced some observers that the interior
designs of most New York apartments were incongruous with the exterior environment. As one writer of the
period noted:

6
Paul T. Frankl, *New Dimensions* (New York:
Payson and Clarke, 1928), 17.

Obviously, in this day of bobbed hair, short skirts, and skyscraping apartments, it is not entirely in the picture of things to turn from contemplating a Babylonian sky-line and be faced by a Directoire sofa. . . . The modern city is not a romantic place. It is something peculiar to itself, and its life has as much right to create its styles as has any period.[7]

In order to bring the aesthetics of the modern city into the home, many designers, some of whom were also architects (cats. 48, 49), looked to the urban environment as a model for forms and ornamentation. The legs of furniture were often designed as straight shafts terminating in small inverted setbacks (cat. 51). The stepped-back masses of skyscraper architecture determined the outlines of case pieces, chairs, and complete decorative ensembles, as in the studio apartment designed by Ilonka Karasz (fig. 4). Some objects, such as Ruth Reeves's "Manhattan" textile pattern, were composite portraits of the city (cat. 47).

Paul Frankl's furniture designs involved a close replication of the skyscraper forms that were changing the face of the metropolis in the late 1920s (cat. 46). Frankl also wrote compelling explanations of the skyscraper's relevance to domestic design:

Some architects call this spirit in our new architecture the spirit of democracy, others call it the result of the machine age, . . . but these variations are only in name. The modern skyscraper is a distinctive and noble creation. It is a monument of towering engineering and business enterprise. . . . Decorative arts and furniture design are already under the powerful modern architectural influence. This can only resolve into one thing: a decorative art that is in keeping with the country and the people who live in it. It will resolve into an American decorative art, original and at the same time satisfying.[8]

Frankl saw the skyscraper as an ideal source for new concepts in modern design that could overcome America's traditional artistic dependence on Europe.

Other designs inspired by the skyscraper were generally less literal than Frankl's. Kem Weber captured the verticality of New York architecture with more abstract yet equally compelling furniture (cat. 50). In other designers' work, such as the veneers on Herbert Lippmann's chair (cat. 52), the ornamentation evokes the New York skyline.[9] Smaller, mass-produced objects, such as the tea service by the Wilcox Silver Plate Company (cat. 54), brought the skyscraper form into the home at more affordable prices than the custom-made furniture of Frankl, Weber, and Lippmann.

Designers were also influenced by changing domestic and social patterns in New York City during the late 1920s. In 1925 the Victorian mansion of William K. Vanderbilt was demolished, an event symbolizing the end of an era when palatial single-family residences lined New York's fashionable Fifth Avenue.[10] With improved automobile and rail transportation, wealthy Manhattanites could build suburban homes as their main residences and maintain relatively small apartments in the city. In response to new demands for smaller urban housing, two-and-a-half miles of fashionable apartment buildings were erected on Park Avenue from Forty-sixth to Ninety-sixth Streets.[11] Apartment living for these tenants and for the less prosperous in other parts of the city often meant adapting to smaller quarters with less or no domestic help.

7
"Modern Art in a Department Store," *Good Furniture Magazine* 30 (January 1928): 35.

8
Frankl, *New Dimensions,* 56–57.

9
Herbert Lippmann to Alan Moss. Information courtesy Alan Moss.

10
John Vredenburg Van Pelt, *A Monograph on the William K. Vanderbilt House* (New York, 1925), 13–18.

11
Christopher Tunnard and Henry Hope Reed, *American Skyline* (Boston: Houghton Mifflin, 1955), 213–14.

These practical considerations strongly affected modern decorative arts and increased the need for compact and easily maintained furnishings. Multipurpose furnishings and rooms were characteristic of urban apartments during the era, and space-saving solutions were more common in America than in France, where multipurpose rooms were considered unsuitable for the greater formality of French domestic life.[12]

Changing social values had a direct impact on the decorative arts; Paul Frankl noted an increasingly impersonal character in domestic settings of the 1920s.[13] A social change related to this development was the new status of women, and as one observer commented, "She is not as feminine as she has always been in the past. Our rooms lack the old-fashioned feminine touch; laces and silks and satins have disappeared almost entirely."[14] During this decade more women began to smoke openly, in part because the cigarette habit signified urbane sophistication for both sexes. Stylish modern smoking accessories, such as Wolfgang and Pola Hoffmann's cigarette holder and ashtray (cat. 55) and the Chase Brass and Copper Company's "Smokestack" (cat. 56), enhanced this symbolism. The cocktail party became an increasingly fashionable social event despite Prohibition, replacing more elaborate functions such as receptions, tea dances, and formal dinner parties that required large rooms and domestic help. The glamour of the liquor ritual actually increased during Prohibition, and efforts to conceal personal liquor supplies often resulted in ingenious contraptions. Gilbert Rohde's "Rotorette" (cat. 58) is a multifunctional cellarette with revolving shelves that alternately display and conceal books, glasses, and liquor bottles.

In 1930 one writer credited Prohibition with the invention of a new furniture form: "It was Prohibition which invented a new use for a new piece of furniture—the cocktail table, something with a low center of gravity, not top-heavy, and easily cleaned."[15] Similarly, Donald Deskey claimed that his adoption of plastic materials in furniture design had a direct relationship to Prohibition:

> I used plastics for the first time as a table top in a room I designed for a private client, and chose that material because of its resistance to cigarette burns and because it was the only suitable material that could withstand the alcoholic concoctions of that era.[16]

Deskey's Bakelite table (cat. 76) suited these requirements for durability. Cocktail accessories also were produced employing modern forms and innovative materials. Russel Wright's chromium-plated cocktail shaker (cat. 57) so strongly resembles a sleek, impersonal machine component that its true function is difficult to recognize.

Skyscrapers, new living arrangements, and changing social mores began to convince many style-conscious New Yorkers of the late 1920s that period-revival furnishings were incongruous and unfashionable at a time of such dynamic change. Consequently new demands developed for furnishings and accessories more appropriate to modern life. Designs incorporating images of the city and objects fashioned in sophisticated modern forms satisfied these demands. An eloquent example is Viktor Schreckengost's punch bowl (cat. 61), which portrays the advertising signs, speakeasies, and jazz music that created the syncopated, if frantic, rhythm of New York's night life.[17] This object symbolizes the urban spirit of the decade, an exuberant source for some of the most original designs produced during this era.

12
Penelope Hunter, "Art Deco and American Furniture," (M.A. thesis, Institute of Fine Arts, New York University, 1971), 2.
13
Frankl, New Dimensions, 18.

14
Sexton, Modern Architecture, 94.

15
Oliver Thorne, "The Modern Metal Chair," Home and Field 40 (May 1930): 50.

16
Quoted in E. F. Lougee, "Furniture in the Modern Manner," Modern Plastics 12 (December 1934): 18.

17
Rocky River Public Library, Cowan Pottery Museum, 14.

46 Desk and Bookcase
about 1928
Designed by Paul T. Frankl
(1887–1958)
for Frankl Galleries, New York City
Walnut and blue-green painted wood
H. 83 in. (210 cm), W. 48¾ in. (123.8 cm),
D. 21¼ in. (54 cm)
Provenance: Thanks for the Memories,
Los Angeles, California
Collection of John Axelrod,
Boston, Massachusetts

Paul Frankl's importance as a promoter of
the modern movement in America is
almost equal to the impact of his design
innovations in the late 1920s. For his
books, *New Dimensions* (1928) and *Form
and Re-form* (1930), Frankl took photographs of his own work that emphasized
the dramatic angles and verticality of his
skyscraper bookcases and desks.[1] In the
compartments of these case pieces, Frankl
placed pre-Columbian artifacts and pot-
ted cacti.[2] One reviewer described Frankl's
designs as the "celebrated sky-scraper
type of furniture, which is as American and
New Yorkish as Fifth Avenue itself."[3]

In addition to their symbolic appeal,
Frankl's works fulfilled the need for functional, compact furnishings. One writer
commented:

> Much of the modern art furniture,
> which is above all else suited to the
> urban taste, is built with the idea of
> modern apartment house space
> saving. . . . Bookcases and drawer
> cabinets follow the skyscraper in
> extending their dimensions upward
> rather than laterally. They are tall,
> narrow and possessed of a surpris-
> ing quantity of put-away space.[4]

This case piece has a hinged flap on the
right side that opens to create a writing
surface. The interiors of the compartments,
painted green, provide a variety of storage

spaces. The rhythmic, irregular silhouette
mimics the setback forms of skyscrapers in
the 1920s.

1
Watson, *Interior Decoration,* 27.
2
See illustration, Migennes, "Paul Th.
Frankl," 52.
3
"American Modernist Furniture," 119.
4
"American Modern Art," 174.

47 Textile

"Manhattan" pattern, 1930
Designed by Ruth Reeves (1892–1966)
for W. & J. Sloane, New York City
Block-printed cotton
H. 80¼ in. (203.3 cm), w. 35⅛ in.
(89.2 cm), Repeat 52½ in. (133.2 cm)
Printed on selvage, "Manhattan Designed
by Ruth Reeves for W. and J. Sloane"
Estate of Ruth Reeves

"That America need not look across the
water for inspiration in textile design is
proved by a glance at the work of Ruth
Reeves," wrote one critic in 1930.[1]
Although inspired by modern French textiles in style and technique, Reeves turned
to native sources for the subject of this pattern. In "Manhattan" she portrays the
Statue of Liberty, Trinity Church penned in
between towering Wall Street skyscrapers,
factories, bridges, airplanes, ocean liners,
switchboard operators, and elegantly
dressed party-goers—a medley of images
that epitomizes modern life in New York
City. The "Manhattan" pattern was printed
in various color schemes—black against a
green background in this example—and
used for wall hangings or curtains.

1
"Fanciful Fabrics Designed Especially for
Country Houses," *Country Life* (U.S.) 59
(December 1930): 46. Source courtesy
W. Scott Braznell.

48 Table
about 1931
Designed by Raymond M. Hood
(1881-1934), New York City
Black glass, steel, wrought iron, brass, and
brass-plated steel
H. 29⅞ in. (75.9 cm), W. 29¹⁄₁₆ in.
(73.8 cm), D. 22⅞ in. (58.1 cm)
Alan Moss Studios, New York City

Raymond M. Hood designed some of the
most powerful icons of the New York skyline, such as the American Radiator, Daily
News, and McGraw-Hill buildings. Hood
studied architecture at the Massachusetts
Institute of Technology (1903) and at the
Ecole des Beaux-Arts in Paris. He initially
designed in various revival styles, but by
the late 1920s he worked in a more modern idiom. He was a participant in the
Metropolitan Museum's "The Architect
and the Industrial Arts" exhibition in
1929; the furniture Hood designed for this
show revealed his characteristically
flamboyant style.[1]

    The vertically stacked disks of this
table evoke associations with symbols of
the machine age such as radio antennas.
A prevalent design motif around the end of
the decade (cats. 50, 59), the disks give the
table a futuristic profile. The shape of the
legs, an abstracted quiver and arrow
motif, and the contrasting gold- and black-
colored materials evoke eighteenth-century French furniture.[2] Although made for
the 1931 Brooklyn showroom of Rex Cole
(a firm that retailed General Electric refrig-
erators), this table would have complemented some of the more daring domestic
interiors of the period.[3]

     1
See Hood's apartment house loggia from
"The Architect and the Industrial Arts"
exhibition, illustrated in Meikle, *Twentieth
Century Limited,* 28.
     2
Compare a table by Jean-Henri Riesener
of the 1770s, illustrated in Claude Frégnac,
et al., *French Cabinetmakers of the Eight-
eenth Century* (New York: French and
European Publications, 1965), 189.
     3
For period illustrations, see Arthur Tappan
North, *Raymond M. Hood* (New York:
Whittlesey House, 1931), 101, and Stern,
Hood, 64.

Table

about 1928–1929
Designed by Ely Jacques Kahn
(1884–1972), New York City
Walnut, quarter-sawn rosewood, and
Formica; maple
H. 23 in. (58.4 cm), w. 29¹⁵/₁₆ in. (76 cm),
D. 17¹⁵/₁₆ in. (45.6 cm)
Penciled on base, "2949"; labeled on
underside, "FORMICA / FOR FURNITURE
FIXTURES / THE FORMICA INSULATION CO. /
4614 SPRING[illegible] / CINCINNATI OHIO"
Collection of Diane Wolf, New York City

Ely Jacques Kahn was one of the most
important and prolific urban architects in
America during the late 1920s. He was
responsible for the design of thirty buildings in New York City from 1925 to 1931.
Born in Manhattan (he was the brother of
Rena Rosenthal), Kahn graduated from the
architecture school of Columbia University
in 1907 and then studied at the Ecole des
Beaux-Arts in Paris where he received a
degree in 1911. He taught design at Cornell University in 1915.[1] Although interested in new architectural developments,
Kahn maintained a flexible attitude toward
stylistic options and placed great emphasis on personal expression:

> The artist will develop his personal-
> ity through qualities in his own mind
> which make him different from his
> confreres. One man will enjoy the
> simple, flat, undecorated surfaces
> which are so characteristic of much
> of the modern architecture in
> Europe; another man will prefer the
> playfulness of form which demon-
> strates some whimsy or phantasy
> on his part.[2]

Kahn was typical of modern American
architects during this period in not adopt-
ing one standardized design aesthetic.

Kahn's reputation as an architect
brought him many interior design commis-

sions. One patron chose his work over
Paul Frankl's because she felt that Kahn
created more livable modern interiors.[3]
This table was made for the library of Frederick Rose's Park Avenue apartment. The
table's fluted pedestal is a modern adaptation of classical architecture but the Formica top identifies it as a product of the
modern age.[4]

1
Robinson and Bletter, *Skyscraper Style,*
16–17; Arthur Tappan North, *Ely Jacques
Kahn* (New York: Whittlesey House,
1931), 5.
2
Quoted in North, *Kahn,* 21.
3
Mrs. Maurice Benjamin to author, conversation, 11 December 1982. Mrs. Benjamin
commissioned interior designs from Kahn
in 1929.
4
See Sexton, *Modern Architecture,* 63, for
period illustration. See also "Apartment
Interiors," *Good Furniture and Decoration*
36 (March 1931): 146. Compare the support on this table with a design by Charles
Thiebaut, a French exhibitor at the Paris
Exposition. See Imprimerie Nationale,
Office Central d'Editions, *Encyclopédie
des arts décoratifs and industriels modernes,* 4: pl. XXI.

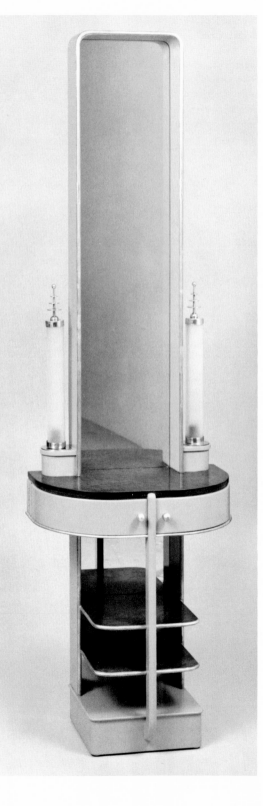

50 Side Table

with Mirror and Electric Lights, about 1929
Designed by Kem Weber (1889–1963),
Hollywood, California
Burl walnut, glass, silvered and painted
wood, and chromium-plated metal; maple
and cedar
H. 75⅜ in. (186.4 cm), w. 22⅝ in.
(57.5 cm), D. 12¼ in. (31.1 cm)
Labeled in side left drawer with metal
plate, "KEM WEBER"
Collection of George H. Waterman III

Glass Table
about 1929
Designed by Kem Weber (1889–1963),
Hollywood, California
Glass and silvered bronze
H. 18¾ in. (47.6 cm),
DIAM. 21¾ in. (55.3 cm)
Collection of George H. Waterman III

Born in Berlin, Karl Emanuel Martin (Kem) Weber was apprenticed to Eduard Schultz, the Royal Cabinetmaker at Potsdam, in 1904, and then studied with Bruno Paul at the Kunstgewerbeschüle in his native city from 1908 to 1910. While Weber was designing the German section of the Panama-Pacific Exposition in San Francisco, World War I broke out. Unable to return to Germany, he remained in the United States. Although he continued to find commissions, he was unable to work in a modern idiom due to postwar anti-German prejudice. By 1926 the cultural climate was more receptive to modern design, and Weber thereafter applied his innovative ideas to both commercial and domestic interior design.[1]

Weber published numerous articles on the strengths and weakness of the new movement. In a piece titled "What About Modern Art?" he denounced department store stylists who had just recently "got on the '*art moderne*' bandwagon" and chided the public for believing that modern design "is really nothing but a succession of triangles in black glass with silver."[2]

Weber lived in California throughout the 1920s, but his impact on the New York design world was as great as if he had been a Manhattan resident. He participated in many major design exhibitions of the period. An innovator in multifunctional furniture, Weber was considered one of the most successful designers for modern apartment living.

These tables are characteristic of the work Weber showed in New York. The pieces originally belonged to a bedroom suite executed for a San Francisco apartment.[3] The elongated proportions of the side table and the setback details on the legs of the glass table mimic features of 1920s skyscrapers; the electric lights crowned with stacked disks are especially evocative of the machine age. The sage green painted surfaces contrast brilliantly with the rich, red wood. Drawers on the side table swivel sideways to open.

1
Gebhard and Von Breton, *Kem Weber,* 37–40.
2
Kem Weber, "What about Modern Art?," *Retailing* 1 (23 November 1929): 20.
3
See period illustration in Ira B. Gorham, "Comfort, Convenience, Color," *Creative Art* 7 (October 1930): 251.

52 Armchair

about 1929
Designed by Herbert Lippmann
(1889–1978?), New York City
Walnut veneer; upholstery not original
H. 32½ in. (82.5 cm), w. 30⅜ in. (77.1 cm),
D. 31¾ in. (80.6 cm)
Collection of George H. Waterman III

Herbert Lippmann trained as an architect
at Columbia University. With Henry C.
Churchill he designed the Lowell apartment house on East Sixty-third Street in
1926. For this building the architects commissioned decorative metalwork from
Walter von Nessen and Edgar Brandt.[1]
Lippmann was also responsible for the
design of several houses with their furnishings in the Manhattan suburbs.[2]

Lippmann's furniture was often as
architecturally inspired as Paul Frankl's
better-known skyscraper designs. His use
of veneers is similar to Viennese work of
the period. On this chair he aimed to repli-
cate the skyline of Manhattan in the figure
of the wood.[3] The inverted setbacks on the
feet also suggest skyscraper architecture.
The chair's cubical form relates to the low,
boxy chairs then popular in France.[4]

1
Robinson and Bletter, *Skyscraper Style,*
15–16.
2
See Sexton, *Modern Architecture,* 73–75.
3
Herbert Lippmann to Alan Moss. Information courtesy Alan Moss.
4
Compare a chair by Jean-Jacques Adnet,
illustrated in Holme and Wainwright, *Decorative Art 1929,* 133. For a period illustration of Lippmann's chair, see Sexton,
Modern Architecture, 114. The original
upholstery was unpatterned.

53 Mantelpiece

between 1925 and 1928
Designed by Jules Bouy (1872–1937),
for Ferrobrandt, Inc., New York City
Wrought iron
H. 77¾ in. (197 cm), w. 62 in. (157.5 cm),
D. 9 in. (21.8 cm)
The Metropolitan Museum of Art, Gift of
Juliette B. Castle and Mrs. Paul Dahlstrom,
1968. 68.70.2

A native of France, Jules Bouy established
his first interior decoration firm in Belgium.
He moved to New York City around the
time of World War I and became associated with L. Alavoine and Company from
1924 to 1927. The Paris-based firm provided modern and period-revival furnishings for fashionable Manhattan
residences, such as the Worgelt apartment, now partially installed in the Brooklyn Museum. During these years Bouy was
also head of Ferrobrandt, Inc., which produced his own designs as well as selling
metalwork by Edgar Brandt (cat. 3). By
1928 he was president and art director of
his own firm, Bouy Inc., and received commissions from such fashionable New Yorkers as Lizzie Bliss and Agnes Miles
Carpenter.[1]

About the time of the Paris Exposition, Bouy designed modern reinterpreta-
tions of eighteenth-century furniture, like
many of his Parisian contemporaries. This
mantelpiece, however, employs more
hard-edged forms indicative of the
machine age. The ornamental setbacks at
the sides evoke the urban architecture of
the period.[2]

1
Obituary, *New York Times,* 29 June 1937,
p. 22; *American Art Annual,* 1930, p. 511.
2
For period illustration, see Juliette Brossard, "Art Moderne," *Talk of the Town* 6
(April 1930): 19.

54 Tea Service

"Diament" pattern, about 1928
Designed by Gene Theobald
for the Wilcox Silver Plate Company
of the International Silver Company,
Meriden, Connecticut
Silver-plated nickel silver with white metal
mounts; replated
Tray, L. 13½ in. (34.3 cm)
Marked on underside, "WILCOX S.P. CO.
[in an arch]/EPNS/INTERNATIONAL S. CO."
Collection of John Axelrod, Boston,
Massachusetts

In this striking mass-produced ensemble,
the tray holds a pot, sugar bowl, and creamer in an architecturally inspired arrangement of masses with stepped-back
silhouettes. The geometric profile and
quarter-circle handles relate to the work of
the French silversmith Jean Puiforcat (cat.
65).[1] American manufacturers rarely publicized the designers of their products during this period (see cat. 67), but Gene
Theobald was credited with the design of
this tea service in a 1929 issue of *Creative
Art*.[2]

1
Compare illustration in Holme and Wainwright, *Decorative Art 1929,* 178.
2
See *Creative Art* 3 (December 1928): I, for
illustration. Theobald is credited in the next
issue, 4 (January 1929): xxii. No information on the designer's dates has been
found. See also Katharine Morrison
McClinton, *Art Deco: A Guide for Collectors* (New York: Clarkson N. Potter, 1972),
176.

5 Cigarette and Match Holder with Ashtray
about 1930
Designed by Wolfgang Hoffmann
(1900– ?) and Pola Hoffmann (b. 1902)
for Early American Pewter Company,
Boston, Massachusetts
Pewter
H. 1¹⁵⁄₁₆ in. (5 cm), w. 4 in. (10.2 cm),
D. 2³⁄₁₆ in. (5.6 cm)
Marked on underside, ''[tower-shaped
monogram composed of letters w, P, O,
and H]/253/HOFFMANN PEWTER/MADE BY/
EARLY AMERICAN/PEWTER COMPANY''
Alan Moss Studios, New York City

The son of Josef Hoffmann, Wolfgang
Hoffmann was born in Vienna where he
studied architecture, attended the
Kunstgewerbeschüle, and worked in his
father's office for two years. Pola Hoffmann was born in Poland and presumably
met her husband while also studying under
Josef Hoffmann in Vienna. They immigrated to the United States in 1925 and
immediately became members of vanguard design circles in New York.[1] The
Hoffmanns' marriage and design partner-
ship dissolved in the 1930s.[2]

Pewter became popular as a result of
the colonial revival; by the end of the
1920s even such conservative holloware
producers as the Early American Pewter
Company were experimenting with modern lines. The Hoffmanns designed several
ashtrays for the company that were
included in The American Federation of
Arts' 1930–31 ''Decorative Metalwork
and Cotton Textiles'' exhibition.[3] All of
these designs had asymmetrically
arranged compartments for ashes,
matches, and cigarettes—forms deriving
from modern nonobjective art. These radically simplified, functional-looking objects

were particularly appropriate for up-to-
date smoking accessories, as the smoking
habit was associated with urbane sophistication during that era.

1
Part of the information in this entry was
extracted from Prather-Moses, ''Interna-
tional Dictionary of Women Workers,'' s.v.
''Pola Hoffmann''; Marta K. Sironen, *A
History of American Furniture* (East
Stroudsburg, Pa.: Towse Publishing Co.,
1936), 140–41.
2
Information courtesy Alan Moss.
3
See The American Federation of Arts, *Dec-
orative Metalwork and Cotton Textiles*
(Washington, D.C., 1930), no. 379; also
Leonard and Glassgold, *Annual of Ameri-
can Design 1931,* 81.

56 Cigarette Holder
''Smokestack'' model, about 1933
Manufactured by Chase Brass and
Copper Company, Waterbury, Connecticut
Chromium-plated metal
H. 2 in. (5 cm), w. 3¾ in. (9.5 cm),
D. 2¼ in. (5.7 cm)
Marked on inside of bottom, ''[centaur]/
CHASE USA''
Collection of Glen Bailey, New Haven

Founded in 1876, the Chase Brass and
Copper Company initially produced
industrial wire, pipe, and tubing. In 1930
the company introduced a chromium
housewares line.[1] This cigarette holder,
which sold for one dollar, was one of the
many Chase designs that satisfied the
demand for modern objects at affordable
prices. Smoking and drinking accessories
formed a large portion of the company's
speciality line, with product names—''Aris-
tocrat,'' ''Connoisseur,'' and ''Cosmopoli-
tan''—that were chosen for their evocation
of sophisticated styles of living. In its fluted
detailing, this design represents a continuation of interest in neoclassical form well
into the Depression era.

1
Thomas M. Rosa, ''Chrome Products by
the Chase Brass & Copper Co.,'' in *Chase
Chrome,* comp. and ed. Robert Koch
(Stamford, Conn., 1978), 3.

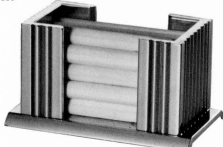

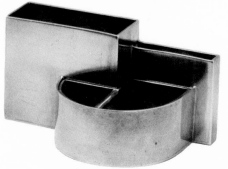

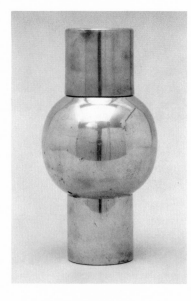

57 Cocktail Shaker
about 1931
Designed by Russel Wright (1904–1976),
New York City
Chromium-plated pewter
H. 9 in. (22.9 cm), DIAM. of top 2¾ in.
(7 cm), DIAM. of center 4⅞ in. (12.4 cm)
Marked on underside, "RUSSEL WRIGHT"
Alan Moss Studios, New York City

In 1930 Russel Wright established a workshop in New York City and began producing informal serving accessories.[1] Wright
showed this design for a chromium-plated
cocktail shaker at the 1931 American
Union of Decorative Artists and Craftsmen
exhibition. One reviewer wrote of it,
"Cylindrical and spherical forms are indicative of the speed of our age."[2] This design
reveals the fascination with sleek industrial
forms that had great symbolic appeal during Wright's era. The shaker would have
been appropriate for sophisticated drinking parties that called for an evocation of
the machine age.

1
"Russel Wright," Russel Wright Archive,
George Arents Research Library, Syracuse
University.
2
Blanche Naylor, "American Design Prog-
ress," *Design* 33 (September 1931): 88.

58 Cellarette
"Rotorette" model, 1929
Designed by Gilbert Rohde (1894–1944),
New York City
Black lacquered wood, leatherette, metal,
and black glass
H. 18¼ in. (46.3 cm), W. 25⅛ in. (63.8 cm),
DIAM. of top 23¾ in. (60.3 cm)
Labeled with a metal plate on underside
of base, "DESIGNED BY / G. ROHDE /
NEW YORK"
Collection of Mr. and Mrs. Lee M. Rohde,
Chappaqua, New York

The son of a cabinetmaker, Gilbert Rohde
wanted to be an architect while growing
up in the Bronx, but his family could not
afford to finance a formal education. After
high school he worked as an apprentice
photographer, newspaper cartoonist, and
advertising illustrator for W. & J. Sloane,
Macy's, and Abraham and Straus. Rohde
visited Paris in 1927, studied French furniture, and traveled to Germany. Returning
to the United States, he set up a workshop
about 1928 and began producing tables
made of chromium-plated metals and
Bakelite. He also received interior design
commissions, such as the highly publicized
Norman Lee penthouse on Sheridan
Square, New York City, that helped establish his reputation.[1]

Rohde installed a "Rotorette" in
the living room of the Lee apartment. The grey-
green leatherette on the sides and the
black glass top were probably chosen for
durability and the glamour associated with
reflective surfaces and synthetic materials
during this period. Reviewers of Rohde's

work especially enjoyed describing the features of this design:

> The open compartment is capacious and deep, capable of holding worthy tomes, . . . the solid foundation of any young man's library. But the touch of the spring—a secret, keyless lock—and lo! two dozen glasses of suggestive size and shape turn slowly into view; again the touch of a spring and a *third* and very secret compartment is revealed, the contents of which would stimulate the most sluggish imagination. Suffice it to say that this "Rotorette" of Gilbert Rohde's has a most ulterior motif of functional need as the basis of its design.[2]

The "ulterior motif," of course, was the clever concealment of contraband liquor.

1
Derek Ostergard and David A. Hanks, "Gilbert Rohde and the Evolution of Modern Design, 1927–1941," *Arts Magazine* 56 (October 1981): 100–101. See also David A. Hanks and Derek Ostergard, *Gilbert Rohde* (New York: Washburn Gallery, 1981), unpaginated.
2
Helen Sprackling, "An Apartment in the Twentieth Century Manner," *House Beautiful* 68 (November 1930): 529. See also Robert Murdock, "Modern Furniture Leads a Double Life," *Good Furniture and Decoration* 36 (January 1931): 50.

59 Standing Floor Lamp
about 1928
Designed by Walter von Nessen (1889–1943) for Nessen Studio, Inc., New York City
Brushed chromium-plated brass; cast iron
H. 67 in. (170.2 cm),
DIAM. of top, 13½ in. (34.3 cm),
DIAM. of base, 12¾ in. (32.4 cm)
Marked on underside of feet, "NESSEN/STUDIO/N.Y./N76"
Yale University Art Gallery, Enoch Vine Stoddard, B.A. 1905, and Marie Antoinette Slade Funds. 1982.5

Electric light was not new in the 1920s but was used increasingly throughout the decade for illuminating advertising signs and skyscrapers. Walter von Nessen and other designers responded to the popular fascination with electricity and manipulated interior lighting to create dramatic effects. Borrowing techniques of indirect illumination from theater designers,[1] lighting specialists devised built-in systems as well as freestanding floor lamps that bounced

light off the ceiling. Torchère lamps were popular in both Europe and America.

Most lamps during von Nessen's time mimicked the forms of earlier lighting devices such as candle holders or gas jets.[2] In the late 1920s, however, designers started encasing electric bulbs in more up-to-date fixtures. The fluted columnar pole on von Nessen's lamp relates to classical columns, but the metal disks and the outward-flaring sections of the shade suggest modern machine-made products. The lamp is plated with brushed chromium, a metal widely used in the decorative arts for the first time during this period. Although many novel materials like Bakelite, rayon, and chromium had been developed early in the century, they were used in new ways during the 1920s to symbolize the machine age. Chromium and most plastics were still relatively expensive,[3] and therefore these materials seemed both luxurious and technologically sophisticated to designers and consumers of the era.

1
Norman Bel Geddes, *Horizons* (Boston: Little, Brown, 1932), 136.
2
Sexton, *Modern Architecture,* 104.
3
Geddes, *Horizons,* 136.

60 Rug

"Electric" pattern, 1930
Designed by Ruth Reeves (1892–1966)
for W. & J. Sloane, New York City
Cotton
H. 74⅛ in. (188.3 cm), w. 42⅛ in. (107 cm)
Estate of Ruth Reeves

In the 1920s a new domestic phenomenon
appeared, the radio room. Ruth Reeves's
abstract pattern for this rug, executed in
shades of red, blue, and green, was
designed to complement the "aluminum
furniture which a radio room in the modern
manner seems to demand."[1] This design,
with its jagged forms resembling lightning
bolts, symbolizes electricity in a way similar
to Walter von Nessen's lamp (cat. 59).

1
W. & J. Sloane, *Exhibition of Contemporary
Textiles* (New York, 1930), unpaginated.

61 Punch Bowl
1931
Designed and decorated by
Viktor Schreckengost (b. 1906),
bowl thrown by R. Guy Cowan,
for Cowan Pottery Studio, Rocky River,
Ohio
Glazed porcelain with sgraffito decoration
H. 8 1/16 in. (20.6 cm), DIAM. of lip 13 3/4 in.
(34.9 cm), DIAM. of foot 6 1/4 in. (15.9 cm)
Signed on side, "VIKTOR SCHRECKENGOST";
impressed on underside, "COWAN"
Collection JHS, New York City

The son of a potter, Viktor Schreckengost
studied at the Cleveland Institute of Art
from 1924 to 1929 before he undertook
postgraduate study in Vienna with Michael
Powolny. Schreckengost joined Cowan
Pottery Studio after his return to America in
1930. When Cowan closed in 1931, he
continued making ceramic sculpture and
also designed for large-scale producers of
ceramic tableware, such as the American
Limoges Ceramics Company.[1]
     The humor and satire in Schrecken-
gost's work is meant to undercut the traditional earnestness of "art" ceramics.[2] The
decoration on this bowl depicts cocktail
glasses, dancers, electric lamps, and
skyscrapers. These images and the words
"follies," "cafe," and "jazz," compose a
collage meant to portray New York City on
New Year's Eve. Although produced in the
early years of the Depression, this piece
represents a continuation of 1920s attitudes toward social life. Eleanor Roosevelt
bought several of these bowls for enter-
taining when her husband was governor of
New York.[3] The bowl was available in two
sizes and in a choice of colors, green and
black, or blue and black, as in this
example.

1
Clark, *Century of Ceramics,* 325–26.
     2
Laurence Schmeckebier, *Viktor Schrecken-
gost: Retrospective Exhibition* (Cleveland:
Cleveland Institute of Art, 1976), 5.
     3
Rocky River Public Library, *Cowan Pottery
Museum,* 14.

PROMOTING MODERN DESIGN

In 1930, the designer C. A. Glassgold observed:

> A few years ago it would have been impossible to predict any life for the modern movement of
> design in America. Now it is palpably absurd to maintain that it is just a fad. In the short space of
> six years, America has become acquainted with its international and sturdy character and
> although many Americans who accept and admire the movement are unaware of its long period
> of development on the continent, they are, however, able to realize its present maturity.[1]

Perhaps overestimating the impact of modern design on the entire country, Glassgold accurately assessed
its impact on a sophisticated urban center like Manhattan. By 1928 forty percent of Lord and Taylor's sales
of furnishings were in modern styles.[2] Most New Yorkers could not afford the expensive modern furnishings
available at fashionable retail outlets, yet many attended the numerous department store and gallery
exhibitions of modern design. R. H. Macy and Co.'s 1928 "International Exposition of Art in Industry"
attracted 100,000 visitors in the first week alone.[3] From its virtually unrecognized existence in Manhattan
before 1925, modern decorative art received considerable publicity and public attention within the span of
a few years.

A demand for modern decorative arts, however, did not develop spontaneously. Vigorous promo-
tional campaigns staged by several segments of the design community stimulated interest in design
innovations. New York City department stores, such as Lord and Taylor, R. H. Macy and Co., John
Wanamaker, B. Altman, and Saks Fifth Avenue, were at the forefront of promoting modern furnishings.
Museums in the New York area—the Metropolitan, Newark, and Brooklyn—played an important role.
Journals concerned with the decorative arts—*Creative Art, Good Furniture Magazine*, *The American
Magazine of Art*, and other publications—covered new developments. Organizations, such as the Ameri-
can Union of Decorative Artists and Craftsmen (AUDAC) and the American Designers' Gallery, created
forums for new ideas in a previously unreceptive environment.

A few outlets for modern European design were established in the early 1920s that set precedents for
later enterprises. In 1922 Joseph Urban, as president of Wiener Werkstätte of America, Inc., opened a
showroom at 581 Fifth Avenue that sold imported Austrian goods and displayed his own designs (cat. 62).
Although the venture was publicized, the organization closed at the beginning of 1924.[4] A similar firm,
Ferrobrandt, Inc., distributed Edgar Brandt's work in America (cat. 3). Established before the 1925 Paris
Exposition, the company probably was dissolved by 1928.[5] Some establishments were more long lasting,
however. Rena Rosenthal's studio sold Austrian ceramics (cat. 63) and other modern designs for several
decades. Georg Jensen's firm established a New York retail outlet in 1923 for modern silver (cat. 64) that is
still in business today.

After 1925, the most important model for the successful promotion of modern design was the Paris
Exposition with its nationalistic and commercial aims. The German Werkbunds and other modern movements in Europe were beginning to challenge the longtime status of the French as the premiere producers
of fine decorative arts. In order to insure the dominance of the French displays and bolster the market for
the nation's luxury trades, the organizers of the Paris exhibition excluded German participation.[6]

1
Glassgold, "Design in America," in Leon-
ard and Glassgold, *Annual of American
Design 1931,* 174.

2
Ella Burns Myers, "Trends in Decoration,"
Good Furniture Magazine 31 (December
1928): 293.

3
Nellie C. Sanford, "An International Exhibit
of Modern Art," *Good Furniture Magazine*
31 (July 1928): 15.

4
The date of the establishment of the New
York Wiener Werkstätte is often mistakenly
given as 1919, following Rosenthal and
Ratzka, *Modern Applied Art,* 173. See the
reviews of the showroom opening in the
New York Times, 14 June 1922, p. 19, and
25 June 1922, sec. 2, p. 6. Sources cour-
tesy W. Scott Braznell. See also Leon V.
Solon, "The Viennese Method for Artistic
Display," *The Architectural Record* 53
(March 1923): 266.

5
Ferrobrandt is listed for the first time in the
1925 Manhattan telephone directory but
no longer appears in 1928.

6
Garner, *Twentieth-Century Furniture,* 68.

The commercial motive behind the French enterprise attracted members of the furnishing trades in America. Although the United States did not participate, Herbert Hoover realized the commercial importance of the Exposition and appointed an investigative commission. One hundred and eight members of trade organizations and art guilds visited the exhibition and prepared a report stressing the importance of modern decorative arts. The Hoover commission urged American industry to establish leadership in instituting design innovations, as French manufacturers had done.[7]

Many members of the Hoover commission (the majority were manufacturers of period-revival furnishings) showed a surprisingly positive interest in modern design. This attitude may have been influenced by current economic conditions. Since the beginning of the decade, the standard of living in American cities and suburbs had risen dramatically. The market for electric irons, vacuum cleaners, radios, washing machines and other appliances, extremely limited before 1920, experienced tremendous growth, and the industrial use of novel materials like Pyrex, Bakelite, cellophane, and rayon also created new economic opportunities. By mid-decade production had exceeded demand, particularly for traditional decorative arts, because most American consumers did not buy furnishings frequently.[8] In 1926 *Good Furniture Magazine* reported: "It is no secret that production facilities have for some years been far in excess of market requirements. . . . The market necessary to absorb this greatly increased production capacity has not been realized."[9] In response to overproduction, the decorative arts industries sought ways to stimulate sales.[10] The Hoover commission realized that the modern designs seen at the 1925 Paris Exposition could potentially create new demands from American consumers.

Despite the 1926 Hoover commission report, major American manufacturers were slow to introduce new lines in the decorative arts. The cost of altering mass-production equipment to create new models discouraged experimentation with untried markets. With few exceptions most modern designs before the 1930s were either custom made or produced in small quantities and were therefore priced beyond the means of the average consumer.

Overproduction and underconsumption affected retailers as well as manufacturers, and large department stores experienced decreasing profits as the 1920s progressed. To encourage sales, retailers like Lord and Taylor, Saks Fifth Avenue, and Macy's redecorated their stores in modern styles and hired innovative designers like Donald Deskey, Frederick Kiesler, and Alexander Archipenko to produce striking display windows. Department stores played an important role in influencing public taste.[11] One reviewer wrote of Lord and Taylor's public programs in 1928: "Lacking museums of decorative and industrial art, the forward-looking American department store becomes a powerful educational and cultural factor in the community. Its influence is probably more immediate than that exerted by museums."[12] New York department stores organized exhibitions and lecture series, like Parisian establishments such as Bon Marché, Studium-Louvre, and other fashionable retailers, in an attempt to create larger markets for their goods.

The 1925 Exposition stimulated department stores in this country to promote new developments in the decorative arts. In the summer of 1925 the Altman's window display of modern hand-printed French linens "lent a stunning color note to the avenue," as one viewer observed.[13] Late in 1925 Wanamaker's displayed some furnishings from the Paris exhibition and the large gift shop Ovington's experienced brisk sales of French glass by René Lalique, Emile Gallé, and Daum Frères, at prices from fifty to one hundred

7
Clute, *Treatment of Interiors,* 62; Meikle, *Twentieth Century Limited,* 24; U.S. Department of Commerce, *Report of the U.S. Commission Appointed by the Secretary of Commerce to Visit and Report upon the International Exposition of Modern Decorative and Industrial Arts in Paris, 1925* (Washington, D.C., 1926), 6, 20–23, 36.

8
Gilman M. Ostrander, *American Civilization in the First Machine Age: 1890–1940* (New York: Harper and Row, 1970), 221–27.
9
"Quality Will Prevail," *Good Furniture Magazine* 27 (October 1926): 168.
10
See Lewis Mumford, "Modernism for Sale," *American Mercury* 16 (April 1929): 454, for a critique of the market strategies employed by decorative arts manufacturers.

11
Neil Harris, "Museums, Merchandising, and Popular Taste: The Struggle for Influence," in *Material Culture and the Study of American Life,* ed. Ian M. G. Quimby (New York: W. W. Norton, 1978), 160–63.
12
Helen Appleton Read, *An Exposition of Modern French Decorative Art* (New York: Lord and Taylor, n.d.), 7.

13
"In Metropolitan Markets," *Good Furniture Magazine* 25 (August 1925): 103.

dollars.[14] Saks Fifth Avenue also began selling modern French designs, such as Jean Puiforcat's silver vase (cat. 65).

The first major department store event modeled after the Paris exhibition was Macy's "Art-in-Trade Exposition," held in the spring of 1927. Robert W. de Forest, president of the Metropolitan Museum of Art, collaborated in the organization of this exhibition. "Much as I am interested in bringing art to the museum, I am more interested in bringing good art into the home," he stated, concluding that department stores had a primary responsibility in this endeavor.[15] Lee Simonson, a prominent New York stage designer, directed the exhibition installation, featuring cork walls and movable display panels. The exhibition featured works by both American and European designers, including Jean Puiforcat, Emile Decoeur, Maurice Marinot, Edgar Brandt, Georg Jensen, Jules Bouy, Carl Walters, Henry Varnum Poor, Lydia Bush-Brown, and an entire room installation of skyscraper furniture by Paul Frankl.[16] Hunt Diederich displayed a chandelier almost identical to cat. 21.[17]

More ambitious department store exhibitions followed in 1928. In February Lord and Taylor staged "An Exposition of Modern French Decorative Art" organized by the store's director of fashion and decoration, Dorothy Shaver, with the assistance of Isabelle Crocé and others. The exhibition included 477 works by Süe et Mare, Emile-Jacques Ruhlmann, Jean Dunand, and more than twenty other French artists.[18] Patronized by New York society figures such as Frank Crowninshield, editor of *Vanity Fair*, the exhibition stimulated an immediate demand for modern Parisian furnishings. Lord and Taylor had difficulty keeping up with orders following this event, although an original suite could cost up to $8,000. The store also reproduced (without permission from the original designers) many of the furnishings from the exhibition.[19] The dressing table in cat. 66 is replicated from a French design, probably purchased at Lord and Taylor.

Other important department store exhibitions in 1928 included the Abraham and Straus display, "The Livable House Transformed," under the direction of Paul Frankl.[20] Altman's staged an "Exhibition of Twentieth Century Taste" that was criticized by Lee Simonson for its "air of Parisian luxuriousness . . . essentially unrelated to the American mind that really craves new and simple surroundings in which to live."[21] Macy's second exhibition, the "International Exposition of Art in Industry," was held in May 1928. Simonson again designed the installation, which featured cases decorated with stylized pyramids and radiating lightning bolts (fig. 5). France, Germany, Austria, Italy, Sweden, and the United States were represented, and individual exhibitors included Bruno Paul, Maurice Dufrène, Josef Hoffmann, Vally Wieselthier, Edvard Hald, Kem Weber, William Lescaze, Eugene Schoen, Ilonka Karasz, Peter Müller-Munk (cat. 9), the International Silver Company (cat. 67), Walter von Nessen, Carl Walters, Henry Varnum Poor, Hunt Diederich, Frederick Carder, and the Cowan Pottery Studio. Richard Bach, director of industrial relations at the Metropolitan Museum of Art, wrote of the Macy's show, "This exhibition closes a chapter in the history of contemporary art. The modern style . . . has come to stay."[22]

Department store exhibitions during this era arose from the collaboration of museum professionals, designers, and members of the decorative arts trades who worked to encourage what they felt was more tasteful design in useful objects. To them better design in "industrial art" did not pertain exclusively to mass-produced objects.[23] Charles R. Richards, then president of the American Association of Museums, wrote in 1927:

14
"In Metropolitan Markets," *Good Furniture Magazine* 25 (December 1925): 323–25.

15
"Current Topics of Trade Interest," *Good Furniture Magazine* 32 (March 1929): 116.
16
R. H. Macy and Co., *The Catalog of the Exposition of Art in Trade at Macy's* (New York, 1927), 8–9; see also William Baldwin, "Modern Art and the Machine Age," *The Independent* 119 (9 July 1927): 39.
17
See illustration in John Taylor Boyd, Jr., "The Art of Commercial Display," *The Architectural Record* 63 (January 1928): 62.
18
See the exhibition catalogue, Lord and Taylor, *An Exposition of Modern French Decorative Art* (New York, 1928); see also "French Art Moderne Exposition in New York," *Good Furniture Magazine* 30 (March 1928): 119–22.
19
Isabelle Crocé to author, conversation, 18 January 1983.

20
Nellie C. Sanford, "The Livable House Transformed," *Good Furniture Magazine* 30 (April 1928): 174–76.

21
Lee Simonson, "Modern Furniture in the Department Store," *Creative Art* 3 (November 1928): xviii.

22
Richard F. Bach, "Styles A-Borning: Musings on Contemporary Industrial Art and Decoration," *Creative Art* 2 (June 1928): xxxviii. See the exhibition catalogue, R. H. Macy and Co., *An International Exposition of Art in Industry* (New York, 1928). In this show the pieces of Müller-Munk's coffee service were nos. 6176–6178 and the International Silver Company's examples of the "Northern Lights" pattern were nos. 6254–6255.
23
Meikle, *Twentieth Century Limited,* 19.

Figure 5. 87

Lee Simonson, Exhibition Installation,
"International Exposition of Art in Industry,"
R. H. Macy and Co., 1928.
Reproduced from *The Architectural Record* 64
(August 1928): 140.
Permission courtesy *The Architectural Record*.

The term industrial art . . . relates to the production of things primarily of use in which the effort has been made to introduce the element of beauty. Whether the things are made by hand, or by machine, or both, is a matter of no importance as regards their relation to life.[24]

In other words, the definition of "industrial art" was very broad for most design-conscious individuals prior to the 1930s. In the mid-1920s Le Corbusier and the Bauhaus designers categorically distinguished handcraft from machine production, but this conceptual division would not become definitively established in American design circles for another decade.[25] For the organizers of modern design exhibitions in America during this period, handcrafted items had a place in displays of "industrial art."

In museum circles concern with better design in useful objects began in the nineteenth century. The South Kensington (now the Victoria and Albert) Museum in London served as a model for several major museums established in this country. The Metropolitan Museum of Art's charter of 1870 included a stipulation that the institution should aid "the application of arts to manufacture and practical life." When Richard Bach became director of industrial relations in 1918, this provision became increasingly important to the museum's programs. Bach's approach was influenced by John Cotton Dana, a pioneer in the effort to make museums more responsive to consumers, manufacturers, and retailers. Head of the Newark Museum Association from 1909 to 1929, Dana established a nontraditional art institution responsive to the needs of the industrial community.[26] The Newark Museum staged exhibitions of German Werkbund design in 1912 and 1922. In 1915 an exhibition of New Jersey clay products attracted 50,000 visitors. A selection of works from the Paris Exposition was staged in 1926, and in 1929 an exhibition of decorative metalwork featured designs by Peter Müller-Munk (cat. 68).[27]

Following the Newark Museum's lead, the Metropolitan Museum became a major sponsor of industrial art exhibitions. The museum's annual exhibitions of American industrial art began in 1917 and originally included only entries based on objects in the museum's collections. Soon that restriction was relaxed, and by the tenth annual exhibition in 1926 no copies or reproductions were allowed, indicating a change in the museum's policies toward encouraging more original designs.[28]

In the late 1920s the Metropolitan Museum continued to sponsor innovative contemporary design. The traveling exhibition from the 1925 Exposition, organized by Charles Richards, included objects by most of the major French designers, including a version of Edgar Brandt's fire screen (cat. 3).[29] As a result of the Exposition, the museum also commissioned an example of Emile-Jacques Ruhlmann's work for the permanent collection (see cat. 2).[30] The Edward C. Moore, Jr., Fund, established in 1922, made this purchase and others from the Exposition possible. These objects formed the nucleus of a permanent gallery of modern decorative arts that opened in 1926.[31] An important exhibition of contemporary Swedish decorative arts was held in 1927, featuring Orrefors glass and furniture designed by Carl Malmsten. The museum also began publishing monographs on topics related to industrial art.[32]

In 1929 the Metropolitan Museum staged its eleventh annual exhibition of industrial art. "The Architect and the Industrial Arts," originally scheduled to run for six weeks, was extended for six months due to overwhelming public response.[33] The exhibition consisted of thirteen ensembles designed by eight prominent modern architects: Ely Jacques Kahn, Ralph T. Walker, Joseph Urban, Eugene Schoen, John Wellborn

24
Charles R. Richards, *Industrial Art and the Museum* (New York: Macmillan, 1927), v.

25
Charles E. Jeanneret-Gris [Le Corbusier], comp., *Almanach d'architecture moderne* (Paris: Les éditions G. Crès, 1925), 168–69; Christopher Wilk, "The Bauhaus Workshops: Principles and Products," lecture, 22 May 1982, given at the symposium "Design 1925," Fashion Institute of Technology, New York City.
26
Meikle, *Twentieth Century Limited*, 20.
27
Dean Freiday, "Modern Design at the Newark Museum: A Survey," *The Museum* 4 (Winter–Spring 1952): 1–4; Harold Ward, "A Museum Makes Friends With Today," *American Magazine of Art* 17 (July 1926): 340–41.
28
Richard F. Bach, "Contemporary American Industrial Art," *Design* 33 (January 1932): 207; Metropolitan Museum of Art, *American Industrial Art*, unpaginated. The catalogue states, "Copies of existing pieces have not been included here."
29
For illustration see *Pennsylvania Museum Bulletin* 22 (December 1926): frontispiece.
30
Hunter-Stiebel, *Metropolitan Museum of Art Bulletin*, 24.
31
Penelope Hunter, "Art Deco and The Metropolitan Museum of Art," *The Connoisseur* 179 (April 1972): 273, 277; Meikle, *Twentieth Century Limited*, 24.
32
The series lasted for four issues: Richard F. Bach, *Museums and the Industrial World* (New York, 1926); Gregor Paulsson, *Swedish Contemporary Decorative Arts* (New York, 1927); Richard F. Bach, *Museum Service to the Art Industries* (New York, 1927); Robert W. de Forest, *Art in Merchandise* (New York, 1928).
33
Bach, "Contemporary American Industrial Art," 207. See the exhibition catalogue, The Metropolitan Museum of Art, *The Architect and the Industrial Arts: An Exhibition of Contemporary American Design* (New York, 1929).

Root, Eliel Saarinen, Raymond Hood, and Armistead Fitzhugh. Frank Lloyd Wright was invited to participate but declined.[34] The exhibition emphasized the versatility of contemporary architects in the design of
decorative objects and interiors as well as architectural structures. Each participant custom-designed
every fixture and furnishing in his ensemble, and all the rooms displayed elaborate ornaments and expensive materials. Eliel Saarinen's dining room (fig. 1) was one of the most successful conceptions. The
proportions and detailing on his flatware (cat. 69) complemented the furniture, textiles, and wallpaper in
the ensemble. Greatly lauded by visitors, the exhibition represented an important chapter in the Metropolitan Museum's patronage of modern design.

A few observers, however, criticized the lavish displays. Douglas Haskell compared the rooms
unfavorably to the 1927 German exposition of housing in Stuttgart that included buildings by Le Corbusier,
Ludwig Mies van der Rohe, and Walter Gropius. He commented on the American exhibitors in the museum
exhibition:

> The architects here have failed in imagination. Instead of envisioning the idea, Industrial Art, 1929,
> they have simply followed the other groups of interior decorators and the department stores in
> arranging one more set of fashionable modern rooms. . . . Bow down, bow down, before the
> upper middle classes—and pray that the good strokes in design may eventually filter through to
> the rest.[35]

Haskell believed that modern design should be affordable to all consumers, not only the well-to-do, in
order to gain acceptance in this country. With the onset of the Depression, this point of view became
increasingly widespread.

The Metropolitan Museum's twelfth industrial design exhibition in 1931 reflected more austere times.
All the entries were manufactured in multiples or mass-produced rather than custom-designed.[36] The goals
of the museum's industrial art program, however, remained essentially the same. In the 1931 exhibition,
Bach declared that the museum "at every point seeks to aid the designer or the manufacturer . . . who may
see, as wisely he must, a potential improvement of his product (and his business) in the time-tested
economic value of design-quality."[37] The museum's design program sought not only to elevate public taste
but to offer industry a means of increasing profits.

In addition to museums, other arts organizations in New York City staged exhibitions and instituted
educational programs that encouraged the acceptance of modern decorative arts. In 1920 the Art Center
was founded as a clearinghouse for ideas on industrial art. Several organizations were affiliated with the
center, including the Art Alliance of America, the New York Society of Craftsmen, and the Art Directors
Club. With six galleries, the organization held an average of sixty exhibitions a year and had over 30,000
visitors in 1925.[38] As the decade progressed, Art Center exhibitions were increasingly dominated by
modern designs, as were the displays sponsored by the Architectural League of New York and the Art-in-
Trades Club. In 1928 The American Federation of Arts began an annual series of traveling exhibitions
featuring one or two media in the decorative arts. Ceramics comprised the first exhibition, which included
over five hundred entries of modern work from Europe and America.[39] The second annual exhibition

34
R. Craig Miller, introd., "Frank Lloyd Wright
at The Metropolitan Museum of Art," *The
Metropolitan Museum of Art Bulletin* 40
(Fall 1982): 3.

35
Douglas Haskell, "The Architects' Modern
Rooms at the Metropolitan," *Creative Art* 4
(March 1929): xlvii. Although Haskell was
particularly critical of the expense of the
museum installations, the Stuttgart buildings were also quite costly and had little
direct relation to low-cost housing,
according to Barbara Miller Lane. See
her study, *Architecture and Politics in
Germany,* 122.

36
Bach, "Contemporary American Industrial
Art," 208.

37
Ibid., 206.

38
Meikle, *Twentieth Century Limited,* 19–20;
Art Center, New York, *The Art Center and
Industry* (New York, 1926), 5, 7, 15.

39
See exhibition catalogue, The American
Federation of Arts, *International Exhibition
of Ceramic Art* (Washington, D.C., 1928);
see also "Modern Industrial Arts," *American Magazine of Art* 19 (March 1928):
158; Ella S. Siple, "The International Exhibition of Ceramic Art," *American Magazine of Art* 19 (November 1928): 602–19.

presented glass and rugs, and the third and final display in 1930–31 featured cotton textiles and decorative metalwork, including pewter smoking accessories by Wolfgang and Pola Hoffmann (cat. 55), bookends by Russel Wright (cat. 42), and textiles by Ruth Reeves (cats. 34, 47, 60).[40] The Federation's official journal, *The American Magazine of Art*, covered these and other design events in the New York area, bringing modern decorative arts to public attention.

Other publications were important in the dissemination of modern design. Popular magazines, such as *Vanity Fair*, *Vogue*, and *Town and Country*, and trade journals like *Good Furniture Magazine*, *The Upholsterer and Interior Decorator*, and *Wallpaper* shifted in the last few years of the 1920s from illustrating only period-revival styles to featuring more innovative modern furnishings. The format and graphic design of these journals reflected changing editorial policies. Sans-serif type, geometric borders, and prismatic backgrounds superseded the Roman type, curlicues, and floral motifs of the pre-1925 period. *Creative Art*, founded in October 1927, provided provocative coverage of New York design events and carried advertisements for furniture by Ilonka Karasz, Eugene Schoen, and Paul Frankl. Books by Edwin Avery Park—*New Backgrounds for a New Age* (1927)—and Paul Frankl—*New Dimensions* (1928), *Form and Re-Form* (1930), and *Machine-Made Leisure* (1932)—contributed to the promotion of modern design.

Some modern designers operated commercial outlets that served to familiarize the public with new developments in the decorative arts. Around 1922, Paul Frankl opened his gallery at 4 East Forty-eighth Street that sold his own furniture as well as imported wallpaper and fabrics. By the end of the decade he was one of the most fashionable decorators in New York. Donald Deskey's company, Deskey-Vollmer, Inc., specialized in screens, lighting fixtures (cat. 30), and furniture. Eugene Schoen maintained showrooms at 115 East Sixtieth Street (cat. 71) that displayed modern decorative arts. His architectural firm received important commissions for public buildings, such as the design of the RKO Theater interiors in Rockefeller Center.[41]

In addition to individual businesses, professional organizations were formed to promote modern design. Arts and crafts designers had established the precedent of forming a society to exhibit work of its members. New organizations emerged in the 1920s, such as the American Designers' Gallery and the American Union of Decorative Artists and Craftsmen, that were modeled after European groups like the Wiener Werkstätte, the German Werkbunds, and the Société des artistes décorateurs in France. Many modern American designers during this period were born and trained in Europe, and after immigrating to this country, they wanted to maintain the Continental standards of the design profession. The designer's status in America, however, was little appreciated. In the 1920s, American designers employed by industry rarely received credit for their work; textile artists were not allowed to sign fabric borders, in contrast to French practices, and this lack of recognition prevailed for those working in other media.[42] Organizations of modern designers worked to elevate their professional status in America as well as to promote new aesthetic developments.

One of the most important organizations of the era, the American Designers' Gallery, Inc., was formed to exhibit works exclusively by modern designers in this country. Donald Deskey, Hunt Diederich, Paul Frankl, Wolfgang and Pola Hoffmann, Ilonka Karasz, Henry Varnum Poor, Ruth Reeves, and Joseph Urban participated in its premier exhibition in 1928.[43] The exhibition showpiece was a bathroom designed

40
See exhibition catalogues, The American Federation of Arts, *International Exhibition: Contemporary Glass and Rugs* (Washington, D.C., 1929) and American Federation of Arts, *Decorative Metalwork,* cats. 379, 424, 789–90, 792.

41
Krinsky, *Rockefeller Center*, 191–92.

42
Helen E. Anderson, "New Decorative Printed Linens," *Good Furniture Magazine* 33 (August 1929): 77.

43
See exhibition catalogue, American Designers' Gallery, *American Designers' Gallery, Inc.* (New York, 1928); see also Douglas Haskell, "The American Designers," *Creative Art* 3 (December 1928): liii.

by Poor with a life-sized nude depicted on the ceramic tiles of the shower stall. Donald Deskey's room included textiles by Ruth Reeves and his own design for an end table (cat. 76) made of industrial materials.

In the second exhibition of the American Designers' Gallery in 1929, the focus shifted from custom-designed luxury ensembles to less costly interiors. The foreword of the catalogue announced:

> The purpose of this exhibition is to show furniture available at prices the average public can pay, rather than furniture depending for its effectiveness on specialized architectural ensembles. . . . The present exhibition offers the purchasing public the opportunity of acquiring furniture created by American designers at prices usually associated with mass production.[44]

This exhibition featured works by the original members as well as designers who did not participate in the first display, including Wharton Esherick (cat. 72). Despite the attempt to accommodate the average consumer, the American Designers' Gallery did not survive the stock market crash.

Lucian Bernhard, Paul Lester Wiener, and Bruno Paul founded Contempora, Inc., a similarly short-lived organization. Drawing on an international membership that included Paul Poiret, Rockwell Kent, and Vally Wieselthier, Contempora staged an exhibition in 1929 of "harmonized" rooms; all the furnishings in the ensembles were packaged as complete units. Although the organization was highly praised by reviewers, it apparently disbanded within a short time.[45]

The American Union of Decorative Artists and Craftsmen shared many goals with the American Designers' Gallery and Contempora. A larger organization, AUDAC's roster reads like a "Who's Who" of modern American decorative arts during this period. Formed in 1928 "to give direction to contemporary design in America, particularly as it applies to industry," AUDAC was organized to accomplish in America what the Société des artistes décorateurs and the German Werkbunds had achieved in Europe.[46] AUDAC's activities included the publication of the illustrated *Annual of American Design 1931* with provocative essays by Lewis Mumford, Frank Lloyd Wright, Paul Frankl, Norman Bel Geddes, and others. AUDAC also staged two major exhibitions of the work of its members. The first exhibition was held in 1930 at the Grand Central Palace in Manhattan, and a more ambitious event was staged at the Brooklyn Museum in the following year. Two textiles by Ilonka and Mariska Karasz were shown (cats. 27, 33), as well as a cocktail shaker (cat. 57) by Russel Wright. The public thronged to see this exhibition, described by one writer as presenting "a definitely national style, suited to contemporary life in the United States, and not copied from European modes."[47] The Brooklyn exhibition was the last major event sponsored by AUDAC, however, which fell victim to the deepening economic crisis of the 1930s.[48]

If short lived, the accomplishments of AUDAC and other organizations of American designers were very real. Within a few years these groups produced alternatives to period-revival furnishings, and along with the organizers of department store and museum exhibitions they helped elevate the status of the design profession in America. If the stock market crash had not occurred, these artist-run cooperative organizations might have had more influence over the course of modern design in this country. The Depression determined another direction, however, for the successful designers of the next decade who collaborated as individuals with American industry.

44
American Designers' Gallery, *American Designers' Gallery, Inc.* (New York, 1929), unpaginated; see also Shepard Vogelgesang, "Contemporary Interior Design Advances," *Good Furniture Magazine* 32 (May 1929): 229–34.

45
See exhibition catalogue, Contempora, *Contempora Exposition of Art and Industry* (New York, 1929); see also Walter Rendell Storey, "Making Modern Rooms 'All of a Piece,'" *New York Times Magazine*, 7 July 1929, pp. 16–17.

46
"Decorative Artists Form Union," *The Architectural Record* 64 (August 1928): 164.

47
Naylor, "American Design Progress," 82. See also Leonard and Glassgold, *Annual of American Design 1931*, 132–33; the catalogue of the Brooklyn exhibition, American Union of Decorative Artists and Craftsmen, *AUDAC Exhibition* (New York: Brooklyn Museum, 1931); and Elizabeth Hamlin, "The Audac Exhibition," *The Brooklyn Museum Quarterly* 18 (July 1931): 93–97.

48
Rosenthal and Ratzka, *Modern Applied Art*, 186.

62 Table

about 1920
Designed by Joseph Urban (1872–1933),
Yonkers, New York
Black lacquered and silvered wood, silk,
and glass
H. 23⅞ in. (60.6 cm), w. 16 in. (40.6 cm),
D. 16 in. (40.6 cm)
The Metropolitan Museum of Art, Emil
Blasberg Memorial Fund, 1978.
1978.492.1

Joseph Urban studied at the Imperial
Academy of Fine Arts (1890–1893) with
Karl von Hasenauer and at the Polytechni-
cum in his native city of Vienna. Urban first
came to the United States for a short time
to design the Austrian pavilion for the 1904
Louisiana Purchase Exposition in St. Louis,
Missouri, for which he won a gold medal.
In 1911 he returned to the United States
permanently, beginning his American
career as a designer for the Metropolitan
Opera and the Ziegfeld Follies in New
York. One of his most striking architectural
designs, the New School for Social
Research (1929–30), stands on West
Twelfth Street.[1]

This table was used in the New York
showroom of the Wiener Werkstätte. In
1922 Urban served as the president of this
short-lived retail outlet of the Austrian
organization. The table's striking contrasts
of dark and light colors, applied spheres,
and rectilinear forms were features of Wiener Werkstätte furniture from the founding
of the organization in 1903.[2] The original
silk top displays the curvilinear floral forms
used by Wiener Werkstätte artists during
the 1920s.[3]

1
The American Federation of Arts, *American
Art Annual,* 1933, 396; Dorothee Müller,
Klassiker des modernen Möbeldesign
(Munich: Keyser, 1980), 152–53.
2
Compare a Josef Hoffmann table illus-
trated in Maurizio Fagiolo dell'Arco,
*Hoffmann: I Mobili Semplici, Vienna,
1900–1910* (Rome: Emporio Floreale,
1977), unpaginated.
3
For period illustration, see Frankl, *Form
and Re-form,* 78.

63 Ceramic Sculpture

before 1929
Designed and executed by
Vally Wieselthier (1895–1945)
for Wiener Werkstätte, Vienna, Austria
Lead-glazed earthenware
H. 17½ in. (44.4 cm), w. 6 in. (15.2 cm),
D. 4⅛ in. (10.5 cm)
Incised on bottom, "485/MADE IN AUSTRIA/
vw [conjoined]/[Wiener Werkstätte
monogram]/7"
Collection of Muriel Karasik Gallery,
New York City

Valerie (Vally) Wieselthier studied under
Michael Powolny at the Kunstgewerbeschüle in Vienna and later headed the
ceramic workshop of the Wiener Werkstätte. Her first exhibition was in Germany
in 1922, and she won a gold and a silver
medal at the 1925 Paris Exposition. Wieselthier came to New York City as a permanent resident in 1929. She showed at The
American Federation of Arts ceramic exhibition (1928–29) and with Contempora,
Inc. She also had exhibitions at the Art
Center in 1928 and at the Weyhe Galleries
in 1930.[1] A reviewer described her
ceramics as "spontaneous, skillful, joyous
work combined with gay color and without
fuss or worry over the usual potter's con-
cerns for texture, detail or finish."[2] Wiesel-

thier also produced designs for glass,
textiles, papier-mâché department store
mannequins, and the metal elevator doors
for Ely Jacques Kahn's Squibb Building
(1929–30) in New York City.[3]

Although designed before Wieselthier immigrated to America, this figurine
with a daring blue and orange costume
embodies the spontaneity characteristic of
the ceramist's later work in this country.
Figures like this one, handmade but produced in multiples by the Wiener Werkstätte, were marketed internationally. In
New York Austrian ceramics were available at Rena Rosenthal's gallery, and from
1922 to 1923 at the Wiener Werkstätte
showroom.

1
Obituary, *New York Times,* 3 September
1945, p. 23; Artist file, "Vally Wieselthier,"
Art Division, New York Public Library;
Clark, *Century of Ceramics,* 339.
2
Ruth Canfield, "The Pottery of Vally Wiesel-
thier," *Design* 31 (November 1929): 104.
3
Extracted from Prather-Moses, "Interna-
tional Dictionary of Women Workers," s.v.
"Vally Wieselthier."

64 Bowl

before 1929
Manufactured by Georg Jensen
Sølvsmedie A/S, Copenhagen, Denmark
Sterling silver
H. 5¼ in. (13.3 cm), w. 14¾ in. (37.5 cm),
D. 11⅛ in. (28.2 cm),
WT. 65.61 oz. (1800 gms)
Marked on underside, "Georg Jensen" in
a crowned circle, and "GJ 925 / #954-306A."
Engraved on underside of foot, "To my
wife Genevieve Wertheim Wasser from
Edwin Wasser, January 10, 1929,
Winifred"
Collection of Ruth and Seymour Geringer

Georg Jensen (1866–1935) established
his Copenhagen silversmithy in 1904, and
the firm quickly gained an international
reputation for high-quality products. By
the time that Jensen's designs were featured at the 1925 Paris Exposition, his work
was already admired in this country by
both the public and American silversmiths.
William Randolph Hearst bought most of
Jensen's silver displayed at the 1915 Panama-Pacific International Exposition.[1] The
firm exhibited in late 1922 at the Art Center,
and by 1923 Jensen had opened a retail
outlet at 159 West Fifty-seventh Street.[2] The
output of this Danish establishment had a
great stylistic impact on both handcrafted
and mass-produced silver in this country.[3]

Jensen employed a large number of
artists to design and execute silver pieces.
The openwork pedestal and naturalistic
ornament of the bowl is typical of the company's output before 1930, but research
has not yet uncovered the individual
designer. This piece belonged to the Wasser family, Manhattan residents who probably purchased it from Jensen's New York
store. At that time the firm was only a retail
outlet for work that was executed in
Denmark.

1
Renwick Gallery, *Georg Jensen Silversmithy* (Washington, D.C.: Smithsonian
Institution Press, 1980), 9, 16.
2
Art Center, New York, *Bulletin of the Art
Center* 1 (November 1922): 58; 2 (November 1923): 98, advertisement. Sources
courtesy W. Scott Braznell.
3
Renwick, *Georg Jensen,* 7.

65 Vase

1927–28
Designed by Jean Puiforcat (1897–1945),
Paris, France; retailed by Saks Fifth
Avenue, New York City
Sterling silver and glass
H. 14¾ in. (37.8 cm),
DIAM. 7¼ in. (18.3 cm)
Marked on edge of base,
"jean e. puiforcat / france / saks fifth
avenue"
Collection of Sydney and Frances Lewis

The greatest French silversmith of the twentieth century, Jean Puiforcat first began
showing his work in 1922. He designed silver with a system of ideal proportions
derived from classical tradition.[1] This vase
also incorporates the disjunctive planes
and deliberate formal ambiguity of nonobjective sculpture in the 1920s. The precious
silver material, however, places the object
within the French tradition of luxurious
decorative arts.

Fashionable Parisian goods were
available at Saks Fifth Avenue and other
New York department stores in the late
1920s. Catering to a wealthy Manhattan
clientele, these stores encouraged a taste
for modern design through the sale of
objects such as this vase.

1
For an illustration of Puiforcat's elaborate
working drawings, see Hillier, *Art Deco,*
41.

6 Vanity and Bench

about 1931

Manufactured for Lord and Taylor,
New York City

Red lacquered wood and chromium-
plated metal

Table, H. 31¼ in. (79.3 cm), W. 41⅜ in.
(105.1 cm), D. 22 in. (55.9 cm)

Bench, H. 19¾ in. (49.5 cm), W. 21⁹⁄₁₆ in.
(54.8 cm), D. 12⅜ in. (31.5 cm)

Cooper-Hewitt Museum, The Smithsonian
Institution's National Museum of Design,
Gift of Mr. James M. Osborn.
1969.97A & B

The Lord and Taylor and Macy's exhibitions in the late 1920s created a demand
for modern furnishings primarily within
affluent, fashionable circles. Mr. and Mrs.
James Osborn, who originally owned this
vanity and bench, were undoubtedly influenced in their choice of furnishings by
these kinds of events. Mr. Osborn recalled
at the time the vanity was given to the
Cooper-Hewitt Museum that the custom-
made piece was commissioned from Lord
and Taylor.[1] Much of the modern furniture
sold at Lord and Taylor was reproduced
from French originals; this object closely
replicates a vanity by Léon Jallot exhibited
at the 1928 Paris Salon d'Automne.[2] The
eccentric forms of the Osborn piece, composed of oblique planes and finished with
red lacquer, would have appealed only to
the most adventurous patrons of the
period.

Prior to her marriage to James
Osborn on 20 November 1929, Marie-
Louise Montgomery had closely followed
modern developments in the decorative
arts. Before the wedding she wrote to her
mother:

> I intend ordering tomorrow [furni-
> ture] for the bedroom at Lord and
> Taylor. . . . I want to get something
> that is really unusual and somehow
> expresses my personality. . . . It has
> to be handmade, for that reason it
> will never become common or be
> seen around in shops like so much
> of this modern furniture. The
> designs are also unusual, although
> not too bizarre . . . I imagine [the
> furniture] will be about 1200
> [dollars].[3]

The practices of Lord and Taylor, Macy's,
and other New York department stores
and manufacturers caused many French
designers to refuse to participate in American design exhibitions in order to avoid
unauthorized reproduction of their work.

1
Notation on the object's loan record at the
Brooklyn Museum.
    2
See illustration in Kahle, *Modern French
Decoration,* 37.
    3
Marie-Louise Montgomery to Mrs. J. F.
Montgomery, undated letter [1929], Mr.
and Mrs. James Marshall Osborn Papers,
The Beinecke Rare Book and Manuscript
Library, Yale University.

67 Bowl

"Northern Lights" pattern, "Spirit
of Today" line, 1928
Designed by Alfred G. Kintz (?–1963)
for Simpson, Hall, Miller and Company
of International Silver Company,
Meriden, Connecticut
Sterling silver
H. 2¹¹⁄₁₆ in. (6.8 cm), w. 11¹¹⁄₁₆ in. (29.6 cm),
DIAM. of base 4½ in. (11.4 cm),
WT. 12 oz. 11 dwt. (390 gm)
Marked on underside, "INTERNATIONAL/
[plumed knight's helmet over a
shield enclosing 'S']/D105A"
Private Collection

In 1928 the International Silver Company
introduced a line of modern tableware
called "Spirit of Today." According to a
promotional brochure issued by the company, the "Northern Lights" pattern, part
of the "Spirit of Today" line, was taken
from a painting by Rockwell Kent.[1] The spi-
raling, linear border decoration gives a
modern, abstract quality to this design and
represents an important departure for
International in the late 1920s from their
usual output of period-revival silver. As
was frequently the practice of large decorative arts manufacturers in this country,
Alfred G. Kintz, the designer of the object,
was not credited in International's promotional material. The "Spirit of Today"

designs, die stamped and mass produced,
were moderately priced.

A winged luncheon plate and com-
pote in the "Northern Lights" pattern were
in the Macy's 1928 "International Exposition of Art in Industry." In the catalogue's
preface, Robert W. de Forest wrote
optimistically:

The leadership which the Macy's
department store in New York has
assumed so successfully becomes
of real interest to Americans. . . .
The department store exerts a profound influence on the sources of
production. It is to be expected that
the manufacturers will therefore
take their cue from the interest of
these retail centers and will antici-
pate the trend towards design
which will catch the spirit and
rhythm of modern life.[2]

1
A copy of the promotional brochure is in
the International Silver Company Historical
Collection, Meriden, Conn. Source courtesy W. Scott Braznell.
2
Macy, *Art in Industry*, 5–6.

68 Bowl

about 1929
Designed and executed by Peter Müller-Munk (1904–1967), New York City
Sterling silver
H. 2½ in. (6.4 cm), DIAM. 8½ in. (21.5 cm), WT. 21 oz. 10 dwt. (666.2 gm)
Marked, "HANDWROUGHT/STERLING SILVER/925/1000C/P [encircled]/PETER MULLER MUNK"
The Newark Museum, U.S. 29.472

This bowl was purchased by the Newark Museum from its exhibition, "Modern American Design in Metal," held in 1929. The show also included a fire screen by Hunt Diederich, smoking stands by Gilbert Rohde, and lamps by Deskey-Vollmer, Inc. Although the Newark Museum staged many exhibitions of modern design during this period, few of the objects displayed were purchased for the permanent collection. The acquisition of this piece departed from usual museum policy. Lack of direct patronage was characteristic of museums sponsoring industrial arts exhibitions. These institutions saw themselves primarily as intermediaries between artists and industry rather than as collectors of modern design.

The use of arches as rim decoration is unusual in silver design. Although they suggest a pattern of repeated "M"s, the first letters of Müller-Munk's compound name, precedents for this kind of decoration exist in Scandinavian and German architecture.[1]

1
See, for example, the Main Hall of the Stock Exchange, Amsterdam, by Henrik Peter Berlage, illustrated in Reyner Banham, *Theory and Design in the First Machine Age* (Cambridge, Mass.: MIT Press, 1980, first published 1960), 169.

69 Model for a Knife

1929
Designed by Eliel Saarinen (1873–1950) for International Silver Company, Meriden, Connecticut
Sterling silver
L. 9¼ in. (23.4 cm), WT. 4 oz. 3 dwt. (129 gm)
International Silver Company Historical Collection

Eliel Saarinen, in his association with the Cranbrook Academy of Art, exerted a great influence in this country on the decorative arts as well as on architecture. From 1893 to 1897 he studied painting at the University of Helsingfors in his native Finland and architecture at the Polytekniska Institute. Saarinen's work was well known in Europe and in the United States before he immigrated to this country in 1923. His first American post was as visiting professor of architecture at the University of Michigan (1923–24), and in 1925 he began developing the Cranbrook educational center in Bloomfield Hills, Michigan. As president of the Cranbrook Academy of Art, he put his personal stamp on one of the most influential centers of art education in America.[1]

The International Silver Company executed this knife model for Saarinen's dining room in the Metropolitan Museum exhibition "The Architect and the Industrial Arts." The knife displays architecturally inspired ornamental setbacks on the handle. The short blade was considered a striking innovation in 1929, and Saarinen filed an application for a patent on the idea. The design facilitated cutting by allowing the index finger to apply pressure on the handle rather than the edge of the blade. In an International Silver Company promotional release, Helen Ufford wrote about Saarinen's short-blade knives, "They make one feel, when using them, like a cosmopolite, and as if the process of eating were now a far more civilized procedure than heretofore." International Silver used the short blade design in several commercially successful silverplate patterns.[2]

Saarinen's association with the International Silver Company and several other metalwork producers fulfilled the goal of the Metropolitan Museum's industrial art program. The museum fostered the collaboration of artist with manufacturer, and this union brought higher profits to business and more up-to-date products to the home.

1
Christ-Janer, *Eliel Saarinen,* 127–30.
2
Information courtesy Edmund P. Hogan, Archivist, International Silver Company. Copies of the press release and Saarinen's patent application are in the International Silver Company Historical Collection, Meriden, Conn.

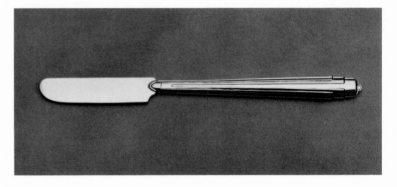

Textile

"American Scene" pattern, 1930
Designed by Ruth Reeves (1892–1966)
for W. & J. Sloane, New York City
Block-printed cotton
H. 105½ in. (268 cm), w. 47¼ in. (120 cm),
Repeat 56 in. (142.2 cm)
Printed on selvage, "'American Scene'
Designed by Ruth Reeves for W and J
Sloane"
Estate of Ruth Reeves

In December 1930 W. & J. Sloane, a
retailer of period-reproduction furnishings,
exhibited twenty-nine textile designs commissioned from Ruth Reeves, including
"American Scene," "Figures with Still Life"
(cat. 34), "Manhattan" (cat. 47), and
"Electric" (cat. 60). Called a "noble experiment" by *Art Digest*, the Sloane commission was represented at The American
Federation of Arts' "Decorative Metalwork
and Cotton Textiles" exhibition.[1] Available
in a choice of color schemes, the designs
were executed in thirteen kinds of cotton
cloth. Sloane's patronage of modern
design represented a significant departure
for the company.

The "American Scene" pattern, executed in shades of green, lavender, and
blue, is an example of Reeves's approach
to textile design, a method that recorded
personal experiences using a modern,
painterly design idiom.[2] Each figure in this
work represents someone in the artist's circle of family and friends.[3] One of the chess
players may be a portrait of Reeves's longtime associate, Maurice Heaton.[4] The
woman at the table with a cat on her lap is
a self-portrait.

1
"Ruth Reeves Performs 'Noble Experiment'," *Art Digest* 5 (15 December 1930):
21; W. & J. Sloane, *Contemporary Textiles*,
unpaginated.
2
Anderson, "Ruth Reeves," 24.
3
Information courtsey Duny Katzman.
4
Information courtesy Maurice Heaton.

71 Design for Iron Door

about 1927
Designed by Lee Schoen (b. 1907),
for Eugene Schoen, Inc., New York City
Pencil on tissue
H. 27⅛ in. (68.8 cm), w. 17¾ in. (44.2 cm)
(sight measurement)
Signed lower right, "Drawn by Lee
Schoen"
Alan Moss Studios, New York City

At establishments like Frankl Galleries and
Eugene Schoen, Inc., the setting was
almost as important in the promotion of
modern design as the objects for sale. This
design, by Eugene Schoen's son Lee
Schoen, was influenced by Edgar Brandt's
ironwork, such as the fire screen (cat. 3)
and the doors for Cheney Brothers. Lee
Schoen joined his father's firm as a fulltime
associate in 1929 after graduating from
Cornell University.

The door for Schoen's showroom at
115 East Sixtieth Street was executed after
this design and provided an elegant introduction to the two-story galleries. Eugene
Schoen's monogram is at the righthand
side of the door. Schoen operated the decorative arts showroom until the early 1930s
when the establishment closed due to the
Depression. Eugene and Lee Schoen,
however, continued to maintain their architectural and interior design practice at 43
West Thirty-ninth Street.[1]

1
Lee Schoen to author, conversation, 13
May 1983.

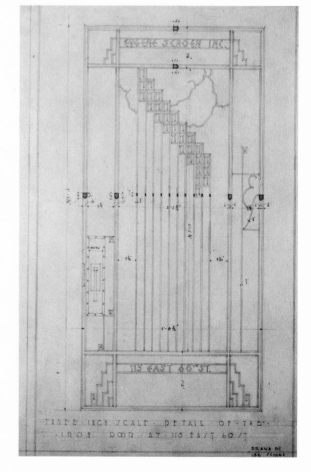

72 Desk Chair

1929
Designed and executed by
Wharton Esherick (1887–1970),
with the assistance of John Schmidt
Padouk, walnut, and leather
H. 25¾ in. (70.5 cm), w. 18 in. (45.7 cm),
D. 18 in. (45.7 cm)
Carved on front underside of seat,
"Wharton Esherick/1929/JS"
Wharton Esherick Museum, Esherick
Family Collection

Wharton Esherick enrolled in the Philadelphia School of Industrial Arts in 1907 and
studied at the Pennsylvania Academy of
the Fine Arts two years later. He lived and
worked in relative seclusion for most of his
career in a studio in Paoli, Pennsylvania. In
1919 he began carving wood to produce
sculpture and furniture. By the mid-1920s
Esherick had become involved with avant-
garde theater and gained familiarity with
German expressionist stage sets. From this
source, as well as from cubism and Frank
Lloyd Wright's furniture, he derived the
oblique angles and triangular motifs of this
chair.[1] Carefully crafted out of exotic
padouk, the object has its original laced-
leather seat and is typical of the rustic yet

aesthetically sophisticated qualities of
Esherick's work.

In 1929 Esherick exhibited this chair
with a desk in New York City at the American Designers' Gallery.[2] Here individuals
like Esherick and Henry Varnum Poor (cats.
35, 36), who used traditional techniques
and materials, exhibited with designers like
Donald Deskey (cat. 76), who worked with
industrial processes. Their common pur-
pose was to promote modern forms in decorative design, and according to Deskey,
they felt no contradiction in displaying their
work together.[3]

1
The Wharton Esherick Museum, *The Wharton Esherick Museum: Studio and Collection* (Paoli, Pa., 1977), 3–8.
2
See American Designers' Gallery, *American Designers' Gallery* (1929), cat. 13.
3
Donald Deskey to author, conversation,
27 April 1983.

73 Shelf Clock
1928–32
Manufactured by Manning, Bowman and
Company, Meriden, Connecticut
Chromium-plated metal and plastic
H. 9¾ in. (24.7 cm), W. 10¼ in. (26 cm),
D. 3¾ in. (9.5 cm)
Stenciled on face, "MANNING-BOWMAN";
stamped on back, "MANNING-BOWMAN &
CO./MERIDEN, CONN. U.S./K904/5a [in a
rectangle, overstruck]"; scratched on
back, "3393FL"
Yale Univeristy Art Gallery, Gift of Jane
Ritchie in Memory of Andrew C. Ritchie.
1981.53.12

This clock appeared in the 1930 catalogue
of Manning, Bowman and Company, and
was advertised as "conservatively modern
in design, yet [harmonizing] perfectly with
the most extreme modernistic setting."[1] The
fluted metal case provides a neoclassically
inspired framework for the radiating
beams on the dial face, a popular design
motif of the era (fig. 5). The black plastic
resembles ebony and gives this object a
sleek elegance. Although mass produced,
this clock was the most expensive in the
company's line, selling for sixty-five dollars. Despite the company's promotional
efforts to appeal to both conservative and
adventurous tastes, this design, like several other innovative models introduced
during this period, was unpopular with
consumers and was dropped from production within a few years.[2]

1
Manning, Bowman and Company,
*Manning-Bowman Synchronous Motor
Clocks* (Meriden, Conn., 1930), 18.
2
Information courtesy Edmund P. Hogan,
Archivist, International Silver Company.

DESIGN FOR INDUSTRY

The Great Depression had dramatic consequences for the modern design movement in New York, as it had for almost every sphere of American life. October 1929 marks the beginning of the Depression era, although several months passed before the full effects of the stock market crash were felt. Many of the most ambitious building projects instituted in the prosperous 1920s, such as the Chrysler and Empire State buildings, were still being completed in the early Depression years. Once finished, they stood half-empty for lack of tenants. The expansion of Manhattan's skyline gradually subsided because few skyscrapers, except for those in the Rockefeller Center complex, were begun in the 1930s.[1]

Most of the objects in this section date from the transitional years at the beginning of the Depression. During this period New York designers gradually shifted away from creating custom-made objects inspired by historical models or the new urban environment. In the 1930s, they began to focus more on mass-produced designs, and their work was increasingly influenced by the machine aesthetic, a stylistic idiom that drew upon the sleek, impersonal forms of industrial products. This fundamental shift was determined by decreasing demand for luxurious, one-of-a-kind objects and by basic transformations in attitudes toward modern design.

Many manufacturers became more conservative at the onset of the Depression. Hollis S. Baker, president of Baker Furniture Factories, Inc., expressed a sentiment that would come to epitomize the backlash against modern design in the early 1930s: "Less speculation and jazz and a little more interest in the home is what the furniture business needs."[2] Some companies and department stores discontinued their modern lines introduced in the late 1920s and returned to promoting only period-revival styles, yet they were still forced to lower their prices dramatically in order to move their stocks. By the spring of 1931 retail furniture prices were fifty percent lower than in 1927.[3]

Despite this crisis in the decorative arts industries, for Walter Dorwin Teague, George Sakier, Russel Wright, and Norman Bel Geddes, and other designers who had the opportunity and were willing to design for industry, the 1930s were extremely successful and lucrative. These individuals were members of the new industrial design profession that evolved from a long tradition of concern for better design in useful objects. Product design in large manufacturing companies was usually the responsibility of staff engineers; a new development in the 1920s was the emergence of a professional class of freelance design consultants. These industrial designers came from widely divergent backgrounds: theater design, advertising, illustration, and engineering. Geddes is credited with opening the first industrial design office in New York City in 1927,[4] but the new profession was not fully established until the Depression.

During the 1930s, hard-hit manufacturers looked to industrial designers to provide attractive new designs that would reverse their diminishing profit margins. Pragmatic manufacturers realized that whenever two products were equal in utility and price, the one that looked more attractive to the purchaser would sell first. Geddes frankly described the market strategy behind many industrial designs: "The artist's contribution touches upon that most important of all phases entering into selling, the psychological. He appeals to the consumer's vanity and plays upon his imagination."[5] Industrial designers, however, not only repackaged existing products to generate greater sales appeal but also were concerned with developing more functional, efficient products. Raymond Loewy redesigned a radio that increased sales for the Colonial Radio Company by 700 percent. A new design in 1933 for an oil heater by Teague brought 400 percent greater sales to the American Gas Machine Company.[6]

1
Krinsky, *Rockefeller Center,* 11.

2
"Special News Bulletin," supplement to *Good Furniture and Decoration* 33 (November 1929): 2.

3
"Seen and Heard in the Trade," *Good Furniture and Decoration* 36 (April 1931): 224.

4
Sheldon Cheney and Martha Candler Cheney, *Art and the Machine* (New York: McGraw-Hill, 1936), 55. When referred to by his last name, the designer preferred "Geddes" to "Bel Geddes," although the latter was used frequently. Meikle, *Twentieth Century Limited,* n. 29, 216.

5
Geddes, *Horizons,* 222.

6
"Both Fish and Fowl," *Fortune* 9 (February 1934): 98.

A few furniture manufacturers, some on the verge of bankruptcy, introduced modern lines to stimulate demand for new furniture. Gilbert Rohde convinced several companies to implement his ideas for space-saving, inexpensive, and multifunctional furniture. His work for Herman Miller, Inc., and the Troy Sunshade Company contributed to the financial stability of these firms during the Depression. By 1939 the Heywood-Wakefield Company had sold 250,000 of Rohde's design for an easily assembled and inexpensive bentwood side chair (cat. 75).[7] Geddes also designed furniture for large-scale manufacturers, and his bedroom suites for The Simmons Company (cat. 78) were modern additions to the firm's more traditional lines of furniture.

Tableware and glassware producers also hired industrial designers to improve their products. The Chase Brass and Copper Company commissioned prominent designers, such as Russel Wright and Walter von Nessen, to create inexpensive and useful objects for the home out of the company's stockpile of parts.[8] The Chase Company promoted its line of chromium-plated tableware as an inexpensive alternative to traditional silver objects. Many of the firm's designs were both aesthetically and commercially successful, such as von Nessen's elegant "Diplomat" coffee service (cat. 80). The Fostoria Glass Company employed George Sakier to create designs (cat. 81) that approached the classic simplicity of Steuben's handmade glassware (cats. 8, 12, 13). Sakier, however, designed Fostoria glassware to be produced in greater quantities than Carder's or Teague's tableware, and the company sold its products at more affordable prices than Steuben.

The work of industrial designers had great appeal during the Depression because it embodied a compelling machine-age symbolism. Industrial designers created futuristic forms reflecting their optimistic belief that technology could one day mass produce enough inexpensive goods to fulfill the needs of all consumers.[9] Behind much of their new, geometrically simplified designs was the desire to create forms that both facilitated and reflected the most up-to-date manufacturing processes. Designers increasingly employed industrially produced materials, such as Bakelite, Formica, and chromium-plated metals, to create sleek objects that looked mass produced. Walter von Nessen's table (cat. 77), with its unornamented Bakelite surfaces and aluminum supports, conveys a technological symbolism, although the piece was actually hand assembled and produced in limited quantities.

The machine aesthetic was often expressed during the 1930s in streamlined forms influenced by recent scientific experiments in reducing the wind resistance of vehicles. Many American designers embodied the aspirations of the Depression years in horizontal lines and continuous curved surfaces of the streamlined mode, which replaced the dominant verticality and disjunctive forms of the 1920s.[10] In New York, modern domestic interiors no longer looked like the Manhattan skyline but now took on the sleek contours of ocean liners, airplanes, and other high-speed vehicles (fig. 6).

A fascination with transportation also was evident in Europe; Le Corbusier's *Towards a New Architecture* included three chapters on the influence of ocean liners, automobiles, and airplanes in architectural design.[11] Members of the European avant-garde like Le Corbusier used transportation vehicles as models for the development of a restrained, complex, and abstract expression of the machine aesthetic. Their work appealed to a small group of intellectuals during the 1920s and 1930s. In contrast, industrial designers in America produced forms more blatantly symbolic of an optimistic outlook toward technology, and their work was accessible to the general public.

7
Ostergard and Hanks, "Gilbert Rohde and the Evolution of Modern Design," 98, 102–03.

8
R. S. McFadden, "Designers' Ability Salvages Waste," *Design* 35 (September 1933): 20–22, 25.

9
Meikle, *Twentieth Century Limited*, 4, 7–8.
10
Paul T. Frankl, *Machine-Made Leisure* (New York: Harper and Brothers, 1932), 159–60; Cheney and Cheney, *Art and the Machine*, 100–02. For a detailed discussion of 1930s style and its sociological implications, see Meikle, *Twentieth Century Limited*; Donald J. Bush, *The Streamlined Decade* (New York: George Braziller, 1975); and Kathleen C. Plummer, "The Streamlined Moderne," *Art in America* 62 (January–February 1974): 46–54.
11
See Le Corbusier, *Towards a New Architecture*, 81–138. One of Le Corbusier's early International Style buildings, the villa at Poissy-sur-Seine, France, includes subtle, abstract references to features of an ocean liner: forms resembling smokestacks, nautical-looking stair rails, and gleaming white surfaces. References to a vehicle were less easily deciphered in Le Corbusier's work, however, than that of American industrial designers, in which a pencil sharpener could look like a streamlined airplane. See, for example, Meikle, *Twentieth Century Limited*, 115.

Figure 6.
Donald Deskey, Design for the
George and Eleanor Rand Apartment, 1930.
Photograph courtesy Cooper-Hewitt Museum,
The Smithsonian Institution's
National Museum of Design.

Figure 7.
Philip Johnson and Ludwig Mies van der Rohe,
Philip Johnson Apartment, 1930.
Photograph courtesy The Museum of Modern Art.

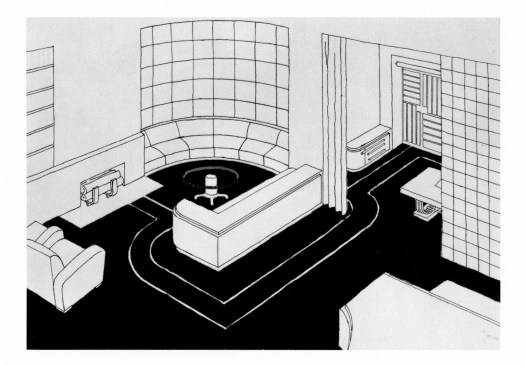

In spite of the different expressions of the machine aesthetic in Europe and America, designers in this country were becoming increasingly aware of the functionalist idiom practiced on the Continent. A machine art exposition in 1927 sponsored by the *Little Review* featured Walter Gropius's work; the translation into English of Le Corbusier's *Towards a New Architecture* (1927), and the publication of Henry-Russell Hitchcock's influential study, *Modern Architecture* (1929), helped introduce International Style theories to New York intellectual circles. The Museum of Modern Art was established in 1929 and immediately became a major tastemaking institution in this country; its exhibitions, such as "Modern Architecture: An International Exhibition,"[12] reflected a predilection for European functionalist design.

Patronage for Bauhaus and other functionalist designers developed in New York in the early 1930s. Philip Johnson, the Museum of Modern Art's first curator of architecture, commissioned Ludwig Mies van der Rohe in 1930 to design the interiors of his New York apartment. The striking two-story living room featured the elegant metal and leather chairs designed by Mies for the German Pavilion of the 1929 Barcelona Exposition (fig. 7). Somewhat paradoxically, Mies's furniture required impeccable handcrafting to produce its machine-made appearance.[13] Alfred H. Barr, Jr., the first director of the Museum of Modern Art, and his wife Margaret began purchasing similar but less expensive American-made tubular steel furniture for their home in 1930. As promoters and patrons of the International Style, Barr, Johnson, and several other scholars and critics called into question the less theoretically rigorous and more commercially motivated modern design in America.

American designers themselves engaged in self-criticism during the early Depression years. Paul Frankl, originally one of the most eloquent admirers of skyscraper form, wrote in 1932: "The skyscraper, considered America's outstanding contribution to the present day civilization, is but a passing fad. The tallest of them, the Empire State, is but the tombstone on the grave of the era that built it." No longer conceiving of Manhattan's tall buildings as cathedrals of commerce, he now declared, "Skyscrapers are monuments to the greedy."[14] Similarly, Donald Deskey labeled much of the post-1925 modern design in America "modernistic," a generally pejorative term by the early 1930s. He wrote in 1933:

> The term "modernistic" . . . was born out of the hysteria created by the Paris Exposition. . . . The grammar of ornament of "modernistic" designers consisted almost exclusively of a few pat motifs such as the zig-zag of lightning, the triangle, the "biche" [doe], and the inverted mouldings of Edgar Brandt.[15]

In the 1930s Deskey, Frankl, and other designers now downplayed their initial enthusiasm for the luxurious designs seen at the 1925 Paris Exposition. Their interest in mass-produced design was frequently stated in terms of functionalist precepts.[16]

In theory and practice, however, most American designers in the early 1930s qualified their approach to European functionalism. In 1930 Frankl questioned the role of function as the sole criterion for determining the form of a design:

12
Hitchcock and Johnson, *Modern Architecture.*

13
Drexler and Daniel, *Twentieth-Century Design,* 43.

14
Frankl, *Machine-Made Leisure,* 140.

15
Deskey, "The Rise of American Architecture," 268.

16
Frankl, *Machine-Made Leisure,* 141–49; Deskey, "The Rise of American Architecture," 268–73.

A bottle is a container constructed to hold a liquid. There are thousands of different shapes of bottles, each of which perfectly fulfills its function. The artist who designs a new type of bottle will derive very little help in this task if he tries to develop form from function alone. . . . Today we are more frank regarding structure, . . . yet frankness and directness do not solely make artists.[17]

Kem Weber's concepts also diverged from the rigorous principles of some of his German colleagues, although he was interested in design deriving from structural considerations. "The furniture of the future should [not] look like hospital appliances," he stated.[18]

A few American designers produced work that conformed to the aesthetics of the International Style. Russel Wright designed many objects in a straightforward, unembellished idiom (cats. 57, 79), although his work was less determined by theoretical considerations than that of functionalists in Europe. Donald Deskey's austere, unornamented designs were exceptional among his American counterparts (cat. 76). In 1928 he created one of the first American-made lines of tubular steel furniture for the Ypsilanti Reed Furniture Company. In this commission he adopted the materials and forms of Bauhaus furniture designs, such as Marcel Breuer's armchair (cat. 74) or Mies van der Rohe's MR chair.[19] Deskey also received an important commission around 1929 from Abby Aldrich Rockefeller for a modern print gallery and boudoir on an upper floor of her West Fifty-fourth Street mansion. This room captured the spacious, hygienic feeling of interior designs by Breuer, Le Corbusier, and other International Style architects.[20] Deskey's work, however, was often closer to the streamlined idiom employed by other industrial designers in America, as in his interior designs for the apartment of George and Eleanor Rand (fig. 6).

Maintaining numerous aesthetic options was a continuing characteristic of American designers' work from the late 1920s to the 1930s. During the Depression, however, new forms were adopted to express the increasing fascination with machine technology. Objects employing aluminum, Formica, Bakelite, and chromium-plated metals were found in increasing numbers in modern living rooms. Even traditional materials, such as glass, brass, and silver, were manipulated in new ways to create sleek surfaces and to suggest an advanced mode of technological production. Within a still generally unsympathetic environment for modern decorative arts, American designers invented compelling symbols of the machine age with the optimistic belief that a brighter future was at hand.

17
Frankl, Form and Re-form, 41, 43.

18
Quoted in Gebhard and Von Breton, Kem Weber, 47.

19
For illustrations of Deskey's designs for the company, see Thorne, "The Modern Metal Chair," 54–55.

20
Information courtesy Donald Deskey. For illustration, see Lougee, "Furniture in the Modern Manner," 18.

74 Armchair

designed 1928, manufactured 1933
Designed by Marcel Breuer (1902–1981),
retailed by Thonet Brothers,
New York City
Chromium-plated tubular steel, painted
wood, and canvas
H. 33½ in. (85.1 cm), w. 21⅞ in. (55.6 cm),
D. 24 in. (61.0 cm)
Wadsworth Atheneum, Hartford,
Purchased about 1934 for use in the Avery
Building of the Wadsworth Atheneum.
1981.106

Inspired by the handlebars of a bicycle he had recently purchased, Marcel Breuer created the first tubular steel chair in 1925 at the Bauhaus. By 1929 several manufacturers, including Thonet Brothers—an Austrian-based firm specializing in mass-produced bentwood furniture—were marketing new tubular steel products;[1] they were still not stock items at New York retail outlets in the early 1930s, however, and few examples survive from this period. Tubular steel furniture was initially quite expensive; an armchair designed by Donald Deskey for the Ypsilanti Reed Furniture Company cost six hundred dollars.[2] This chair was ordered by the Wadsworth Atheneum in 1933 from Thonet's outlet in New York. The Hartford museum was one of the first American institutions to incorporate International Style furnishings into its interiors.

Breuer was born in Hungary and became a student at the Bauhaus in Weimar, Germany, in 1920.[3] The design of this chair evolved from new concepts developed in the late 1920s by Breuer, Mart Stam, and Mies van der Rohe. They discovered that the strength of steel tubing allowed construction of chairs out of continuous curved members, and therefore the back legs could be eliminated. This revolutionary discovery permitted them to incorporate the principle of cantilevered construction into chair design.

The chromium-plated metal supports of chairs served an important symbolic function for designers at the Bauhaus. Although the early chairs incorporating tubular steel were largely handcrafted, their machine-made appearance served as a sign of the fundamental break these designers made with tradition both in materials and construction practices.

1
Christopher Wilk, *Thonet: 150 Years of Furniture* (Woodbury, N.Y: Barron's Educational Series, 1980), 98.
2
Information on the cost of the Ypsilanti Reed chair courtesy Donald Deskey.
3
Wilk, *Breuer,* 15–16.

75 Chair

1930 or 1931
Designed by Gilbert Rohde (1894–1944)
for Heywood-Wakefield Company,
Boston, Massachusetts
Beech with walnut stain, and leatherette
H. 31½ in. (82.1 cm), w. 16 in. (40.6 cm),
D. 21 in. (53.3 cm)
Private Collection

In developing this simply constructed and
inexpensive chair, Gilbert Rohde was
inspired by a long tradition of bentwood
furniture and the early designs of the Finnish architect Alvar Aalto.[1] This design was
first produced by the Heywood-Wakefield
Company, and Rohde later reworked the
chair into slightly different versions for
Herman Miller, Inc., and the Kroehler
Company. Based on clearly defined juxta-
positions of curved and straight lines, the
chair complemented the generally austere
modern interiors of the Depression era.

1
David A. Hanks, *Innovative Furniture in
America: From 1800 to the Present* (New
York: Horizon Press, 1981), 65.

76 Table

about 1928
Designed by Donald Deskey (b. 1894),
New York City
Brass-plated steel, Bakelite, and wood;
lacquer finish not original
H. 17¾ in. (45.1 cm), w. 20 in. (50.8 cm),
D. 12 in. (30.5 cm)
Alan Moss Studios, New York City

This table, shown in the 1928 American
Designers' Gallery exhibition, was also
used in several domestic interiors designed
by Deskey in the early 1930s.[1] The simple
design, with unornamented Bakelite surfaces and brass-plated steel supports,
reveals Deskey's familiarity with Bauhaus
furniture. This piece was custom-made, as
were all of Deskey's designs in the late
1920s.[2] In the 1930s, however, he began
collaborating with large manufacturers
such as the Widdicomb Furniture Company, which mass produced his designs.

1
See installation photograph in "American
Artists' [sic] Gallery" file, Donald Deskey
Archive, Cooper-Hewitt Museum.
2
Information courtesy Donald Deskey.

77 Table
1930
Designed by Walter von Nessen
(1889–1943) for Nessen Studio, Inc.,
New York City
Aluminum, brushed chromium-plated
metal, and Bakelite
H. 18½ in. (46.9 cm), w. 15¼ in. (38.7 cm),
D. 15¼ in. (38.7 cm)
Stamped on underside, "NESSEN/STUDIO/
N.Y./452/NESSEN/STUDIO/N.Y."
The Metropolitan Museum of Art,
Purchase, in Memory of Emil Blasberg,
1978. 1978.492.2

In 1930, when many other businesses were
facing bankruptcy, Nessen Studio
announced its expansion. From a small-
scale supplier to architects and decorators,
it became a general distributor to retailers.[1] Walter von Nessen sustained the
company throughout the Depression with
innovative designs, such as his distinctive
models of swing-arm table and floor
lamps.[2] This table, although more embellished than Donald Deskey's design (cat.
76), is considerably less ornate than either
von Nessen's earlier mirror or floor lamp
(cats. 4, 59). In its Bakelite and aluminum
surfaces and simple rectilinear composition, the table looks forward to von
Nessen's functional-looking work of the
mid-1930s rather than back to his more
historically referential designs of the late
1920s.[3]

1
"Von Nessen Studio Expands Business,"
Retailing 2 (22 March 1930): 17.
2
For illustration, see Drexler and Daniel,
Twentieth-Century Design, 67.
3
For period illustration, see Leonard and
Glassgold, *Annual of American Design
1931,* 68.

78 Vanity Table and Mirror

about 1932
Designed by Norman Bel Geddes
(1893–1958) for The Simmons Company,
Chicago, Illinois
Enameled steel, chromium-plated metal,
and patinated brass; wooden drawer
sides
Table, H. 29½ in. (74.9 cm),
W. 44 in. (111.8 cm), D. 19 in. (48.3 cm)
Mirror, H. 26 in. (66 cm),
W. 27½ in. (69.9 cm), D. 6½ in. (16.5 cm)
Label inside drawer,
"THE SIMMONS COMPANY"
Collection of Mimi Findlay, New Canaan,
Connecticut

Norman Bel Geddes described himself as
"generally self-educated," although he
briefly attended the School of the Chicago
Art Institute.[1] In the 1910s and 1920s he
was a successful advertising artist and
stage designer in New York. He began a
new design career in 1927 by adapting
theater aesthetics to department store window displays.[2] In 1930 Geddes had forty
assistants in his industrial design firm, and
by 1932 he had developed new streamlined designs for trains, automobiles,
steamships, airplanes, theaters, restau-
rants, and factories.[3]

Before the late 1920s American furniture manufacturers sometimes used an
inexpensive material like sheet metal to
imitate more expensive wood veneers.[4]
Geddes was proud of his designs for Simmons because they did not perpetuate the
use of metal as an ersatz substitute for
wood. In 1929 he declared, "In creating
these Simmons designs I have always kept
in mind the medium in which I was working
and believe that the furniture immediately
reveals itself as metal."[5] Geddes's state-
ment articulates the "truth to materials"
design principle espoused by European
functionalists of the time, derived from
design reform movements of the
nineteenth century.

1
Who's Who in American Art, 1940–41, s.v.
"Geddes, Norman Bel."
2
For illustration of his windows, see Meikle,
Twentieth Century Limited, 50–51.
3
"Bel Geddes," *Fortune* 1 (July 1930): 51.
See Geddes, *Horizons, passim,* for illustra-
tions of his streamlined designs.
4
Geddes, *Horizons,* 233.
5
Quoted in "Simmons Co. Offers Suite by
Bel Geddes," *Retailing* 1 (19 October
1929): 2.

**79 Knife, Fork, Soup Spoon, and Salt and
Pepper Shakers**

about 1930
Designed by Russel Wright (1904–1976),
New York City
Sterling silver and stainless steel
Knife, L. 6½ in. (16.5 cm)
Fork, L. 7½ in. (19 cm)
Soup Spoon, L. 6½ in. (16.5 cm)
Salt and pepper shakers, each,
H. 1⅜ in. (3.2 cm), W. 1⅛ in. (2.8 cm),
D. 1⅛ in. (2.8 cm)
The Metropolitan Museum of Art, Gift of
Russel Wright, 1976. 1976.67.52A, .53A,
.54A, .55, .56

Russel Wright, like most of the designers
represented in this exhibition, owed much
to contemporary European ideas. These
flatware prototypes, executed by Wright
himself, may have been put into small-
scale production about 1933.[1] The objects
relate to flatware designs by Jean Puiforcat
and Josef Hoffmann,[2] yet have a straightforward, unembellished quality of their
own. In the design for the cubical salt and
pepper shakers, Wright reduced the
objects to the most basic geometric units.
Underlying the stripped-down simplicity
that characterizes some of the American
design of the era was the desire to develop
easily reproduced forms to facilitate mass
production. Although very elaborate and
ornate designs that resembled handcrafted objects could also be mass produced, the modern designers of this era
increasingly wanted their work to look
machine made.

1
See illustration in *Country Life* (U.S.) 65
(March 1934): 66. Source courtesy W.
Scott Braznell. When Russel Wright gave
this set of flatware to the Metropolitan
Museum, he recalled that he designed it in
1930. The date is given as 1933 in William
J. Hennessey, *Russel Wright: American
Designer* (Hamilton, N.Y.: Gallery Associa-
tion of New York State, 1983), 92.
2
For illustrations, see American Craft
Museum, *For the Table Top* (New York,
1980), 34; and Graham Hughes, *Modern
Silver throughout the World, 1880–1967*
(New York: Crown Publishers, 1967), 176.

80 Coffee Service

"Diplomat" model (Coffee Pot, Creamer,
Sugar Bowl, Tray), before 1931
Designed by Walter von Nessen
(1889–1943) for Chase Brass and Copper
Company, Waterbury, Connecticut
Chromium-plated copper and plastic
Pot, H. 8 in. (20.3 cm),
DIAM. 2⅜ in. (6.7 cm)
Sugar bowl, H. 4 in. (10.1 cm),
DIAM. 2⅜ in. (6.7 cm)
Creamer, H. 2¾ in. (6.9 cm),
DIAM. 2⅜ in. (6.7 cm)
Tray, DIAM. 10 in. (25.4 cm)
Marked on undersides,
"[centaur]/CHASE/USA"
Yale University Art Gallery, Stephen
Carlton Clark, B.A. 1903, Fund.
1982.30 A–D

The individual pieces of this coffee service
are ingeniously and economically made
from one piece of chromium-plated
extruded pipe. The black plastic handles
evoke the feeling of ebony, and the fluted
forms of the service recall the elegance of
handmade neoclassical silver, although
the design probably has a more immediate source in the metalwork of Josef
Hoffmann. This coffee service represents
Walter von Nessen's output as an industrial designer. His designs for the Chase
Brass and Copper Company were much
more widely distributed than were objects
produced in limited editions by his own
firm, Nessen Studio.[1]

1
This coffee service is model no. 17029 in
Chase's 1936–37 catalogue. See Koch,
Chase Chrome, 12. See also "Machinal
Moulds Metal," *Interior Architecture and
Decoration* 37 (December 1931): 274, for
period illustration.

81 Vase
about 1930
Designed by George Sakier (b. 1897)
for Fostoria Glass Company,
Moundsville, West Virginia
Green lead glass
H. 13 in. (33 cm), DIAM. 4½ in. (11.4 cm)
Alan Moss Studios, New York City

Like many of the native New Yorkers represented in this exhibition, George Sakier
studied at Columbia University. He trained
as an engineer but also studied painting
after World War I. As director of the
Bureau of Design for the American Radiator and Standard Sanitation Company, he
created interiors for the New York office
building that Raymond Hood designed for
the company in 1924. Sakier specialized in
bathroom accessories and fittings.[1]

Sakier began working for the Fostoria
Glass Company in the late 1920s.[2] This
vase design was available in many colors
(rose, green, amber, ebony, topaz, and
wisteria) and three different sizes. In a
1934 article Sakier illustrated the design as
an example of his work in the "classic
modern" mode. He conceived of his
designs for bathroom fixtures in a different

spirit, calling them "functional modern."[3]
This simultaneous use of various idioms in
response to individual commissions was
characteristic of American designers who
were dependent on industry to implement
their innovations.

Like Steuben, Fostoria followed the
same trend toward producing colorless
engraved glass in the late 1920s and
1930s. Steuben promoted its products to a
wealthy elite, however, whereas Fostoria
produced modern designs for middle-class
patrons of the Depression era.

1
Who's Who in American Art, 1940–41, s.v.
"Sakier, George."
2
Hazel Marie Weatherman, *Fostoria: Its
First Fifty Years* (Springfield, Mo.: The
Weathermans, 1972), 109.
3
George Sakier, "Primer of Modern
Design," *Arts & Decoration* 40 (November
1933): 36–37. Source courtesy W. Scott
Braznell.

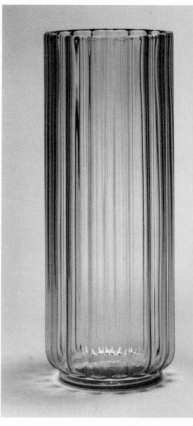

Designers and Manufacturers

M. H. Birge and Sons Company
Buffalo Fine Arts Academy/Albright Art Gallery. *Exhibition of Wall Paper: Historical and Contemporary.* Buffalo, N.Y., 1937.
Copley, Frank W., and Glover, W. H. "The Birge Story." *Niagara Frontier* 6 (Spring 1959): 1–18.

Jules Bouy
Brossard, Juliette. "Art Moderne." *Talk of the Town* 6 (April 1930): 19–22.

Edgar Brandt
Pennsylvania Museum Bulletin 22 (December 1926). Frontispiece.

Lydia Bush-Brown
"Modernistic Wall Hangings." *Good Furniture Magazine* 31 (August 1928): 104–10.
Notebook. "To the Cooper-Hewitt Museum of Design From Lydia Bush-Brown." Collection of the Cooper-Hewitt Museum, The Smithsonian Institution's National Museum of Design, New York.
"Silk Murals for Wall Decorations." *Arts & Decoration* 26 (March 1927): 46.

Edward F. Caldwell and Company
American Magazine of Art 24 (April 1932): 273. Illustration.

Frederick Carder
Gardner, Paul V. *The Glass of Frederick Carder.* New York: Crown Publishers, 1971.
Renwick Gallery. *The Glass of Frederick Carder.* Washington, D.C.: Smithsonian Institution, 1972.

Chase Brass and Copper Company
Koch, Robert, ed. and comp., with Rosa, Thomas M. *Chase Chrome.* Stamford, Conn., 1978.
McFadden, R. S. "Designers' Ability Salvages Waste." *Design* 35 (September 1933): 20–22, 25.

Consolidated Lamp and Glass Company
Paine, Shirley. "Shop Windows of Mayfair." *Garden and Home Builder* 47 (July 1928): 510.
Weatherman, Hazel Marie. *Colored Glass of the Depression Era 2.* Ozark, Mo.: Weatherman Glassbooks, 1974.

Cowan Pottery Studio
Rocky River Public Library. *Cowan Pottery Museum.* Rocky River, Ohio, 1978.

Donald Deskey
Deskey, Donald. "The Rise of American Architecture and Design." *The London Studio* 5 (April 1933): 266–73.
———. "Style in Summer Furniture." *Good Furniture and Decoration* 34 (April 1930): 201–06.
Donald Deskey Archive. Cooper-Hewitt Museum, The Smithsonian Institution's National Museum of Design, New York.
Gratz, Roberta Brandes. "Is Rockefeller Center Losing Its Heart?" *Soho Weekly News,* 12 January 1978, pp. 10–11.
House and Garden 55 (March 1929): 101. Illustration.
Lougee, E. F. "Furniture in the Modern Manner." *Modern Plastics* 12 (December 1934): 18–20, 61–62.

Wilhelm Hunt Diederich
Brinton, Christian. *Hunt Diederich.* New York: Kingore Galleries, 1920.
"Indian Craftwork for Our Homes." *Good Furniture Magazine* 32 (April 1929): 212–18.
Price, F. Newlin. "Diederich's Adventure in Art." *International Studio* 81 (June 1925): 170–74.
"Seen in New York." *Good Furniture Magazine* 25 (September 1925): 132–37.

Wharton Esherick
The Wharton Esherick Museum. *The Wharton Esherick Museum: Studio and Collection.* Paoli, Pa., 1977.

Fostoria Glass Company
Weatherman, Hazel Marie. *Fostoria: Its First Fifty Years.* Springfield, Mo.: The Weathermans, 1972.

Paul T. Frankl
"American Modernist Furniture Inspired by Sky-scraper Architecture." *Good Furniture Magazine* 29 (September 1927): 119–21.
Frankl, Paul T. *Form and Re-form.* New York: Harper and Brothers, 1930.
———. *Machine-Made Leisure.* New York: Harper and Brothers, 1932.
———. *New Dimensions.* New York: Payson and Clarke, 1928.
Migennes, Pierre. "Un Artiste décorateur américain: Paul Th. Frankl." *Art et Décoration* 53 (January 1928): 49–56.

Norman Bel Geddes
"Bel Geddes." *Fortune* 1 (July 1930): 51–57.
Geddes, Norman Bel. *Horizons.* Boston: Little, Brown, 1932.
———. "Streamlining." *Atlantic Monthly* 154 (November 1934): 553–63.
"Simmons Co. Offers Suite by Bel Geddes." *Retailing* 1 (19 October 1929): 2.

Maurice Heaton
"An Illuminated Glass Mural." *Architecture* 66 (December 1932): 351.
Bitterman, Eleanor. "Heaton's Wizardry with Glass." *Craft Horizons* 14 (June 1954): 10–15.
Clute, Eugene. "Craftsmanship in Decorated Glass." *Architecture* 64 (July 1931): 11–16.
"Master Craftsman in Glass." *Interior Design* 28 (September 1957): 146–47.
Naylor, Blanche. "National Alliance of Art and Industry Shows New Design Trends." *Design* 36 (May 1934): 4–5.

Raymond Hood
North, Arthur Tappan. *Raymond M. Hood.* New York: Whittlesey House, 1931.
Stern, Robert A. M., with Thomas P. Catalano. *Raymond M. Hood.* New York: Rizzoli, 1982.

International Silver Company
Creative Art 3 (December 1928): I. Illustration; 4 (January 1929): xxii.
Historical Collection. International Silver Company, Meriden, Conn.

Georg Jensen
Art Center, New York. *Bulletin of the Art Center* 1 (November 1922): 58; 2 (November 1923): 98.
Renwick Gallery. *Georg Jensen Silversmithy.* Washington, D.C.: Smithsonian Institution Press, 1980.

Ely Jacques Kahn
"Apartment Interiors." *Good Furniture and Decoration* 36 (March 1931): 141–48.
Kahn, Ely Jacques. *Design in Art and Industry.* New York: Charles Scribner's Sons, 1935.
———. "Modern Lighting Departs Radically from the Methods of the Past." *House and Garden* 58 (August 1930): 42–47.
———. "The Province of Decoration in Modern Design." *Creative Art* 5 (December 1929): 885–89.
North, Arthur Tappan. *Ely Jacques Kahn.* New York: Whittlesey House, 1931.

Mariska Karasz
"Mariska Karasz." *Interiors* 120 (September 1960): 215.
"Reviews and Previews." *Art News* 53 (October 1954): 59.

Lenox, Inc.
Lenox, Inc. *Lenox China: The Story of Walter Scott Lenox.* Trenton, N.J., n.d.

Erik Magnussen
Carpenter, Charles H., Jr. *Gorham Silver: 1831–1981.* New York: Dodd, Mead, 1982.
"Contemporary Industrial and Handwrought Silver" file, The Brooklyn Museum Archives, Brooklyn, N.Y.
"Silver in Modern Designs." *House and Garden* 52 (November 1927): 106. Illustration.
Storey, Walter Rendell. "Fine Art and Design in New Furnishings." *New York Times,* 28 September 1930, sec. 5, pp. 14–15.
"They Seem to Agree that Gifts Must Be Smart." *The Jewelers' Circular* 101 (November 1930): 82–83.

Manning, Bowman and Company
Manning-Bowman Synchronous Motor Clocks. Meriden, Conn.: Manning, Bowman & Company, 1930.

Peter Müller-Munk
Müller-Munk, Peter. "Handwrought Silver." *Charm* 9 (April 1928): 38–39, 81–83.
———. "Machine—Hand." *Creative Art* 5 (October 1929): 709–12.
Patterson, Augusta Owen. "The Decorative Arts." *Town and Country* 83 (15 April 1928): 70–71, 118, 121.
Read, Helen Appleton. "The Modern Theme Finds a Distinctive Medium in American Silver." *Vogue* 72 (1 July 1928): 58–59ff.

Henry Varnum Poor
Gutman, Walter. "Four Potters." *The Arts* 14 (September 1928): 154–58.
Poor, Henry Varnum. *A Book of Pottery: From Mud into Immortality.* Englewood Cliffs, N.J.: Prentice-Hall, 1958.

Ruth Reeves
Anderson, Harry V. "Ruth Reeves." *Design* 37 (March 1936): 24–26, 39.
"Cotton Printing." *Good Furniture and Decoration* 35 (December 1930): 301–03.
"Fanciful Fabrics Designed Especially for Country Houses." *Country Life* (U.S.) 59 (December 1930): 46–47.
Naylor, Blanche. "Textiles Derived from Paintings." *Design* 33 (February 1932): 214–17, 219.
Reeves, Ruth. "Relation of Modernism to Linen." *Retailing* 1 (5 January 1929): 19.
"Ruth Reeves Performs 'Noble Experiment'." *Art Digest* 5 (15 December 1930): 21.
Sloane, W. & J. *Exhibition of Contemporary Textiles.* New York, 1930.

Gilbert Rohde
Hanks, David A., and Ostergard, Derek. *Gilbert Rohde.* New York: Washburn Gallery, 1981.
Murdock, Robert. "Modern Furniture Leads a Double Life." *Good Furniture and Decoration* 36 (January 1931): 50–53.
Ostergard, Derek, and Hanks, David A. "Gilbert Rohde and the Evolution of Modern Design, 1927–1941." *Arts Magazine* 56 (October 1981): 98–107.
Rohde, Gilbert. "What Is Industrial Design?" *Design* 38 (December 1936): 3–5.
Sprackling, Helen. "An Apartment in the Twentieth Century Manner." *House Beautiful* 68 (November 1930): 484–86, 528–30.

Rookwood Pottery Company
Cummins, Virginia Raymond, comp. *Rookwood Pottery Potpourri.* Silver Spring, Md.: Cliff R. Leonard and Duke Coleman, 1980.
Peck, Herbert. *The Book of Rookwood Pottery.* New York: Crown Publishers, 1968.
Trapp, Kenneth R. *Toward the Modern Style: Rookwood Pottery, the Later Years: 1915–1950.* New York: Jordan-Volpe Gallery, 1983.

Eliel Saarinen
Christ-Janer, Albert. *Eliel Saarinen.* Chicago: University of Chicago Press, 1948.
Cranbrook Academy of Art. *The Saarinen Door: Eliel Saarinen, Architect and Designer at Cranbrook.* Bloomfield Hills, Mich., 1963.

George Sakier
Sakier, George. "Primer of Modern Design." *Arts & Decoration* 40 (November 1933): 36–37.

Eugene Schoen
Downs, Joseph. "A Buffet in the Contemporary Style." *Pennsylvania Museum Bulletin* 24 (March 1929): 19.
Mannes, Marya. "Gallery Notes." *Creative Art* 2 (February 1928): VII–XV.
Sanford, Nellie C. "An Architect-Designer of Modern Furniture." *Good Furniture Magazine* 30 (March 1928): 116–18.
Schoen, Eugene. "The Design of Modern Interiors." *Creative Art* 2 (May 1928): XL–XLIII.
———. "House and Garden's Modern House." *House and Garden* 55 (February 1929): 94–95.
———. "Industrial Design: A New Profession." *American Magazine of Art* 31 (August 1938): 472–79.

Viktor Schreckengost
Schmeckebier, Laurence. *Viktor Schreckengost: Retrospective Exhibition.* Cleveland: Cleveland Institute of Art, 1976.

Steuben Glass
Madigan, Mary Jean Smith. *Steuben Glass: An American Tradition in Crystal.* New York: Harry N. Abrams, 1982.
Steuben Glass. *Masterpieces in Glass by Steuben.* Corning, N.Y., n.d.

Walter Dorwin Teague
Siff, Mary. "A Realist in Industrial Design." *Arts & Decoration* 41 (October 1934): 44–48.
Teague, Walter Dorwin. *Design This Day.* New York: Harcourt Brace, 1940.
———. *Industrial Art and Its Future.* New York: New York University, 1936.

Joseph Urban
Clute, Eugene. "Lighting Made a Part of Architecture in the New School for Social Research." *American Architect* 139 (May 1931): 36–41.
Solon, Leon V. "The Viennese Method for Artistic Display." *The Architectural Record* 53 (March 1923): 266–71.

Walter von Nessen
House and Garden 58 (December 1930): 21. Illustration.
"Machinal Moulds Metal." *Interior Architecture and Decoration* 37 (December 1931): 274–75.
"Von Nessen Studio Expands Business." *Retailing* 2 (22 March 1930): 17.

Carl Walters
"Carl Walters—Sculptor of Ceramics." *Index of Twentieth-Century Artists* 3 (June 1936): 305–6.

Kem Weber
Gebhard, David, and Von Breton, Harriette. *Kem Weber: The Moderne in Southern California, 1920 through 1940.* Santa Barbara: The Art Galleries, University of California, 1969.
Gorham, Ira B. "Comfort, Convenience, Color: Examples from the Designs of Kem Weber." *Creative Art* 7 (October 1930): 248–53.
Grafley, Dorothy. "Kem Weber: Industrial Designer." *Design* 49 (May 1948): 15–16, 22.
"Modern Furniture from Los Angeles." *Good Furniture Magazine* 29 (November 1927): 233–36.
Weber, Kem. "What about Modern Art?" *Retailing* 1 (23 November 1929): 20.
———. "Why Should the American Furniture Buyer, Manufacturer and Designer Go to Europe?" *Good Furniture Magazine* 25 (November 1925): 261.

Vally Wieselthier
Artist File, "Vally Wieselthier." Art Division, New York Public Library.
Canfield, Ruth. "The Pottery of Vally Wieselthier." *Design* 31 (November 1929): 103–05.
Wieselthier, Vally. "Ceramics." *Design* 31 (November 1929): 101–02.

Russel Wright
Country Life (U.S.) 65 (March 1934): 66. Illustration.
Hennessey, William J. *Russel Wright: American Designer.* Hamilton, N.Y.: Gallery Association of New York State, 1983.
Vogue 74 (3 August 1929): 52. Illustration.
Russel Wright Archive. George Arents Research Library, Syracuse University, Syracuse, New York.

Exhibitions

Exposition Internationale des Arts Décoratifs et Industriels Modernes, Paris, 1925
Connick, Charles J. "The Youthful Spirit of France: An Abiding Impression of the Recent Paris Exposition." *American Magazine of Art* 17 (February 1926): 85–89.
Cresswell, Howell S. "The Paris Exposition of Modern Decorative Arts: The Individual Pavilions of Private Firms and Decorators." *Good Furniture Magazine* 25 (October, December 1925): 187–99, 310–17.
Imprimerie Nationale, Office Central d'Editions et de Librairie. *Encyclopédie des arts décoratifs et industriels modernes au XXème siècle.* 12 vols. Paris, 1925. Reprint, New York: Garland, 1977.
"The International Exposition of Modern Decorative and Industrial Art." *Good Furniture Magazine* 25 (September 1925): 121.
Musée des Arts Décoratifs, Paris. *Cinquantenaire de l'Exposition de 1925.* Paris: Presses de la Connaissance, 1976.
Peets, Orville. Letter to editor. *American Magazine of Art* 16 (January 1925): 35.
Read, Helen Appleton. "The Exposition in Paris." *International Studio* 82 (November 1925): 93–97.
Sanford, Nellie C. "The Loan Exhibition from the Paris Exposition Shown in The Metropolitan Museum of Art." *Good Furniture Magazine* 26 (April 1926): 185–88.
Scarlett, Frank, and Townley, Marjorie. *Arts Decoratifs 1925: A Personal Recollection of the Paris Exhibition.* London: Academy Editions, 1975.
United States Department of Commerce. *Report of the U.S. Commission Appointed by the Secretary of Commerce to Visit and Report upon the International Exposition of Modern Decorative and Industrial Arts in Paris, 1925.* Washington, D.C., 1926.
Villa, Georges. "Paris Exposition Shows Way to New Art of Future." *American Magazine of Art* 17 (April 1926): 190–92.
Wright, Richardson. "The Modernist Taste." *House and Garden* 48 (October 1925): 78–79, 110, 114.

American Designers' Gallery, Inc.

American Designers' Gallery, Inc. *American Designers' Gallery, Inc.* New York, 1928. First exhibition catalogue.

———. *American Designers' Gallery, Inc.* New York, 1929. Second exhibition catalogue.

"Exhibit of American Designers' Gallery." *Good Furniture Magazine* 32 (January 1929): 40–45.

Haskell, Douglas. "The American Designers." *Creative Art* 3 (December 1928): lii–liii.

———. "Cheaper, Better Rooms." *Creative Art* 4 (May 1929): xl–xli.

Vogelgesang, Shepard. "Contemporary Interior Design Advances." *Good Furniture Magazine* 32 (May 1929): 229–34.

American Union of Decorative Artists and Craftsmen

American Union of Decorative Artists and Craftsmen. *AUDAC Exhibition.* New York: Brooklyn Museum, 1931.

"Decorative Artists Form Union." *The Architectural Record* 64 (August 1928): 164.

Hamlin, Elizabeth. "The Audac Exhibition." *The Brooklyn Museum Quarterly* 18 (July 1931): 93–97.

"Here and There in New York." *Good Furniture and Decoration* 34 (May 1930): 277–80.

McGregor, Donald. "AUDAC in Brooklyn." *Good Furniture and Decoration* 36 (June 1931): 322–25.

Naylor, Blanche. "American Design Progress." *Design* 33 (September 1931): 82–89.

Contempora, Inc.

Contempora, Inc. *Contempora Exposition of Art and Industry.* New York, 1929.

"Modern Rooms on Display." *New York Times,* 19 June 1929, p. 63.

Read, Helen Appleton, and Haskell, Douglas. "Art and Industry—'Contempora.' " *Creative Art* 4 (June 1929): xviii–xix.

Storey, Walter Rendell. "Making Modern Rooms 'All of a Piece.' " *New York Times Magazine,* 7 July 1929, pp. 16–17.

Department Store Exhibitions

Bach, Richard F. "Styles A-Borning: Musings on Contemporary Industrial Art and Decoration." *Creative Art* 2 (June 1928): xxxvii–xl.

Baldwin, William. "Modern Art and the Machine Age." *The Independent* 119 (9 July 1927): 35–39.

Boyd, John Taylor, Jr. "The Art of Commercial Display." *The Architectural Record* 63 (January 1928): 58–66.

"Cheap and Smart." *Fortune* 1 (May 1930): 82–86, 142.

"French Art Moderne Exposition in New York." *Good Furniture Magazine* 30 (March 1928): 119–22.

"In Metropolitan Markets." *Good Furniture Magazine* 25 (August 1925): 102–07.

"In Metropolitan Markets." *Good Furniture Magazine* 25 (December 1925): 321–26.

Lord and Taylor. *An Exposition of Modern French Decorative Art.* New York, 1928.

Macy, R. H., and Co. *The Catalog of the Exposition of Art in Trade at Macy's.* New York, 1927.

———. *An International Exposition of Art in Industry.* New York, 1928.

"The Macy Exposition of Art in Industry." *The Architectural Record* 64 (August 1928): 137–43.

Read, Helen Appleton. *An Exposition of Modern French Decorative Art.* New York: Lord and Taylor, n.d.

Sanford, Nellie C. "An International Exhibit of Modern Art." *Good Furniture Magazine* 31 (July 1928): 15–20.

———. "The Livable House Transformed." *Good Furniture Magazine* 30 (April 1928): 174–76.

Simonson, Lee. "Modern Furniture in the Department Store." *Creative Art* 3 (November 1928): xvi–xxii.

Small, Peter. "The Modern French Decorative Art Exposition." *Creative Art* 2 (March 1928): xlii–xlv.

Exhibitions of Industrial Art and Modern Design: Museums and Other Arts Institutions

The American Federation of Arts. *Decorative Metalwork and Cotton Textiles: Third International Exhibition of Contemporary Industrial Art.* Washington, D.C., 1930.

———. *International Exhibition: Contemporary Glass and Rugs.* Washington, D.C., 1929.

———. *International Exhibition of Ceramic Art.* Washington, D.C., 1928.

"The Architect and the Industrial Arts: An Exhibition of Contemporary American Design, The Metropolitan Museum of Art." *American Magazine of Art* 20 (April 1929): 201–12.

Art Center, New York. *The Art Center and Industry.* New York, 1926.

Bach, Richard F. "Contemporary American Industrial Art." *Design* 33 (January 1932): 204–8.

———. *Museum Service to the Art Industries.* New York: Metropolitan Museum of Art, 1927.

———. *Museums and the Industrial World.* New York: Metropolitan Museum of Art, 1926.

Colwell, M. W. "Data on Exposition of Bad Taste." Press release of show held at Modernist Studios, New York, 19 April 1914.

De Forest, Robert W. *Art in Merchandise.* New York: Metropolitan Museum of Art, 1928.

Freiday, Dean. "Modern Design at The Newark Museum: A Survey." *The Museum* 4 (Winter–Spring 1952): 1–32.

Haskell, Douglas. "The Architects' Modern Rooms at the Metropolitan." *Creative Art* 4 (March 1929): xlvi–xlix.

Horn, Richard. "MOMA's 'Good Design' Programs Changed Historic U.S. Taste." *Industrial Design* 29 (March–April 1982): 43–47.

Hunter, Penelope. "Art Deco and The Metropolitan Museum of Art." *The Connoisseur* 179 (April 1972): 273–81.

Little Review. Machine Age Exposition. New York, 1927.

The Metropolitan Museum of Art. *American Industrial Art: Tenth Annual Exhibition of Current Manufactures Designed and Made in the United States.* New York, 1926.

———. *The Architect and the Industrial Arts: An Exhibition of Contemporary American Design.* New York, 1929.

———. *Twelfth Exhibition of Contemporary American Industrial Art.* New York, 1931.

"Modern Decorative Arts from Paris at the Metropolitan Museum of Art." *American Magazine of Art* 17 (April 1926): 170–74.

"Modern Industrial Arts." *American Magazine of Art* 19 (March 1928): 157–58.

The Newark Museum Association. *The Clay Products of New Jersey at the Present Time.* Newark, N.J., 1915.

———. *Exhibition of German Applied Art.* Newark, N.J., 1922.

———. *An Exhibition of New Objects from Abroad.* Newark, N.J., 1922.

———. *Notes on Floor Covering.* Newark, N.J., 1931.

Paulsson, Gregor. *Swedish Contemporary Decorative Arts.* New York: Metropolitan Museum of Art, 1927.

Richards, Charles R. "The International Ceramic Exhibition." *Creative Art* 3 (October 1928): xlii–xlvii.

———. "The Second International Exhibition of Industrial Art." *American Magazine of Art* 20 (November 1929): 604–14.

"Settings for Contemporary Industrial Art." *American Architect* 145 (December 1934): 9–11.

Siple, Ella S. "The International Exhibition of Ceramic Art." *American Magazine of Art* 19 (November 1928): 602–19.

Vogelgesang, Shepard. "The Museum and the Architect." *The Architectural Forum* 50 (April 1929): 591.

———. "Toward a Contemporary Art." *Good Furniture Magazine* 32 (March 1929): 117–28.

Wadsworth Atheneum. *Exhibition of Modern Decorative Arts.* Hartford, Conn., 1928.

Walker, Ralph T. "Architecture of To-day: An American Architect's View." *Creative Art* 5 (July 1929): 460–65.

Ward, Harold. "A Museum Makes Friends with Today." *American Magazine of Art* 17 (July 1926): 338–45.

General and Group Studies

Sources Published to 1939

Ackerman, Phyllis. *Wallpaper: Its History, Design and Use.* New York: Frederick A. Stokes, 1923.

The American Federation of Arts. *American Art Annual*: "Directory of Craftsmen and Designers." Washington, D.C., 1930.

"American Modern Art: Its History and Characteristics." *Good Furniture Magazine* 27 (October 1926): 172–74.

Anderson, Helen E. "New Decorative Printed Linens." *Good Furniture Magazine* 33 (August 1929): 77–80.

"Art and Machines." *The Architectural Forum* 60 (May 1934): 331–35.

"Art Moderne Furniture Design in America." *Good Furniture Magazine* 29 (October 1927): 179–82.

"Art Moderne Rugs to the Fore." *Good Furniture Magazine* 31 (September 1928): 140–44.

"The Art Museum and the Store." *Good Furniture Magazine* 24 (March 1925): 142.

Atherton, Carlton. "Design and Changing Ideals." *Design* 35 (February 1934): 7–12.

———. "Speed Determines New Forms." *Design* 35 (April 1934): 4–7.

Bach, Richard F. "Art and the Machine." *American Magazine of Art* 19 (February 1928): 73–77.

———. "Functionalism." *Good Furniture and Decoration* 34 (June 1930): 9, 338.

———. "New Style or Polyglot?" *American Architect* 138 (November 1930): 38–41.

Barr, Alfred H., Jr. "Modern Art Questionnaire." *Vanity Fair* 28 (August 1927): 85, 96, 98.

Bonney, Thérèse and Louise. *Buying Antique and Modern Furniture in Paris.* New York: Robert M. McBride, 1929.

"Both Fish and Fowl." *Fortune* 9 (February 1934): 40–43ff.

Cheney, Sheldon, and Cheney, Martha Candler. *Art and the Machine.* New York: McGraw-Hill, 1936.

Clute, Eugene. "Modern Decorative Light Sources." *Architecture* 64 (August 1931): 71–76.

———. *The Treatment of Interiors.* New York: Pencil Points Press, 1926.

"Color in Industry." *Fortune* 1 (February 1930): 85–94.

"Commercial Art." *American Magazine of Art* 16 (September 1925): 498–99.

"Commercialism in Art." *American Magazine of Art* 15 (February 1924): 92.

"Commercializing Art Moderne Furniture." *Good Furniture Magazine* 30 (January 1928): 30–31.

Crawford, M. D. C. "Primitive Art and Modern Design." *Creative Art* 3 (December 1928): xxxviii–xliv.

Crittall, W. F. "The Manufacturer Replies to the Craftsman." *Creative Art* 3 (November 1928): 307.

"Current Topics of Trade Interest." *Good Furniture Magazine* 32 (March 1929): 115–116, 128.

Dana, John Cotton. "Is a Museum Good for Anything?" *American Magazine of Art* 20 (October 1929): 584.

———. "Museums of Design without Objects." *American Magazine of Art* 19 (August 1928): 433–35.

———. *The New Relations of Museum and Industries.* Newark, N.J.: Newark Museum Association, 1919.

———. *Should Museums Be Useful?* Newark, N.J.: Newark Museum, 1927.

De Forest, Robert W. "Art in Everyday Life: A Radio Talk." *American Magazine of Art* 17 (March 1926): 127–29.

Dreyfuss, Henry. *10 Years of Industrial Design.* New York: Pynson Printers, 1939.

Ferriss, Hugh. *The Metropolis of Tomorrow.* New York: Ives Washburn, 1929.

Finch, Arthur T. "The Place of the Designer in the Ceramic Industry." *American Magazine of Art* 20 (January 1929): 29–35.

Forsyth, Gordon. *20th-Century Ceramics.* London: The Studio, 1936.

Gloag, John. "Wood or Metal?" *Creative Art* 4 (January 1929): 49–50.

Gorham, Ira B. "The Furniture Industry Evidences a Growing Interest in Art." *American Magazine of Art* 19 (August 1928): 444–45.

Green, Kneeland L. "Modern Life, Ordinary Things, Design: Americana Fabrics." *Creative Art* 4 (February 1929): 102–07.

Hale, Frank Gardiner. "The Handicrafts." *American Magazine of Art* 19 (February 1928): 70–72.

Hamlin, Talbot F. "Is Originality Leading Us into a New Victorianism?" *American Architect* 141 (February 1932): 18–19, 70–74.

Haskell, Douglas. "Art in Industry: The Humble Daisy." *Creative Art* 4 (January 1929): li.

———. "A Fine Industrial Design." *Creative Art* 3 (December 1928): l–li.

Hitchcock, Henry-Russell, Jr. *Modern Architecture: Romanticism and Reintegration.* New York: Payson & Clarke, 1929.

———, and Johnson, Philip, et al. *Modern Architecture: International Exhibition.* New York: Museum of Modern Art, 1932.

Hoffmann, Herbert. *Modern Interiors in Europe and America.* New York: William Edwin Rudge, 1930.

Holme, C. Geoffrey, and Wainwright, Shirley B., eds. *Decorative Art 1929.* New York: Albert and Charles Boni, 1929.

Huxley, Aldous. "Notes on Decoration." *Creative Art* 7 (October 1930): 239–42.

Janneau, Guillaume. *Modern Glass.* London: The Studio, 1931.

Jeanneret-Gris, Charles E. [Le Corbusier], comp. *Almanach d'architecture moderne.* Paris: Les éditions G. Crès, 1925.

———. *Towards a New Architecture.* Trans. by Frederick Etchells. London: Architectural Press, 1927.

Johnson, Philip. *Machine Art.* New York: Museum of Modern Art, 1934.

Kahle, Katharine Morrison [McClinton]. *Modern French Decoration.* New York: G. P. Putnam's Sons, 1930.

Kantack, Walter W. "Fundamentals in Providing for Good Lighting." *American Architect* 140 (September 1931): 48–51, 120, 124.

Keppel, Frederick P., and Duffus, R. L. *The Arts in American Life.* New York: McGraw-Hill, 1933.

Kiesler, Frederick. *Contemporary Art Applied to the Store and Its Display.* New York: Brentano's, 1930.

Leonard, R. L., and Glassgold, C. A., eds. *Annual of American Design 1931.* New York: Ives Washburn, 1930.

Levy, Florence N. "Radio Talk: The Museum of Art, How to Use and Enjoy It." *American Magazine of Art* 16 (August 1925): 425–28.

McAndrew, John. "'Modernistic' and 'Streamlined'." *The Museum of Modern Art Bulletin* 5 (December 1938): 2–3.

"Modern Art in a Department Store." *Good Furniture Magazine* 30 (January 1928): 32–35.

"Modern Industrial Arts." *American Magazine of Art* 19 (March 1928): 157–58.

"Modern Interior Lighting." *American Architect* 145 (November, December 1934): 59–72, 53–68.

"Modernism in Industrial Art." *American Magazine of Art* 15 (October 1924): 540–41.

"Modernistic Wall-Paper Designs." *Good Furniture Magazine* 30 (April 1928): 177–78.

Mumford, Lewis. "Art in the Machine Age." *The Saturday Review of Literature*, 8 September 1928, pp. 102–3.

———. "The Economics of Contemporary Decoration." *Creative Art* 4 (January 1929): xix–xxii.

———. "Modernism for Sale." *American Mercury* 16 (April 1929): 453–55.

"Museum Ideals or the Ideal Museum." *American Magazine of Art* 18 (January 1927): 34–35.

Myers, Ella Burns. "Trends in Decoration." *Good Furniture Magazine* 31 (December 1928): 291–94.

Naylor, Blanche. "Design Dominates Rockefeller Center's Unified Decorative Scheme." *Design* 35 (February 1934): 3–6.

"New York—The Nation's Style Pulse." *Retailing* 1 (13 April 1929): 17.

Newark Public Library and The Newark Museum Association. *Design in Industry.* 3 vols. Newark, N.J., May 1930–December 1932.

"The Old and the New." *American Magazine of Art* 20 (November 1929): 640–41.

Park, Edwin A. *New Backgrounds for a New Age.* New York: Harcourt, Brace, 1927.

"Quality Will Prevail." *Good Furniture Magazine* 27 (October 1926): 168.

"Radio Talks on Art." *American Magazine of Art* 16 (March 1925): 147–48.

Raley, Dorothy, ed. *A Century of Progress: Homes and Furnishings.* Chicago: M. A. Ring Co., n.d.

Read, Helen Appleton. "Twentieth-Century Decoration." *Vogue* 71 (1 April 1928): 84–85ff.

Read, Herbert. *Art and Industry.* London: Faber and Faber, 1934.

Richards, Charles R. *Art in Industry.* New York: National Society for Vocational Education and Department of Education of the State of New York, 1922.

———. "In Defense of the Modern Movement in European Industrial Art." *American Magazine of Art* 15 (December 1924): 631–34.

———. "The Development of the Industrial Arts." *American Magazine of Art* 19 (February 1928): 77–78.

———. *Industrial Art and the Museum.* New York: Macmillan, 1927.

Ringel, Fred J., ed. *America as Americans See It.* New York: Harcourt, Brace, 1932.

Rosenthal, Rudolph. "American Industry and the American Artist." *Design* 36 (December 1934): 3–4.

Rourke, Constance. *Charles Sheeler.* New York: Museum of Modern Art, 1939.

Sayler, Oliver M. *Revolt in the Arts.* New York: Brentano's, 1930.

"Seen and Heard in the Trade." *Good Furniture and Decoration* 36 (April 1931): 223–24.

Sexton, R. W. *The Logic of Modern Architecture.* New York: Architectural Book Publishing Co., 1929.

Sironen, Marta K. *A History of American Furniture.* East Stroudsburg, Pa.: Towse Publishing Co., 1936.

Skelley, Leloise D. *Modern Fine Glass.* New York: Richard R. Smith, 1937.

"Special News Bulletin." Supplement to *Good Furniture and Decoration* 33 (November 1929): 1–3.

Storey, Walter Rendell. "American Rugs for the Modern Age." *Creative Art* 9 (July 1931): 42–51.

Thorne, Oliver. "The Modern Metal Chair." *Home and Field* 40 (May 1930): 50–55.

Todd, Dorothy, and Mortimer, Raymond. *The New Interior Decoration.* New York: Charles Scribner's Sons, 1929.

"Tubular Chairs Are the Vogue in Paris." *The Upholsterer and Interior Decorator* 84 (15 April 1930): 104–5.

Van Houghton, Rebecca. "Modern Influences in Interior Decoration." *Town and Country* 70 (20 November 1915): 25–27, 50, 52.

Van Pelt, John Vredenburg. *A Monograph on the William K. Vanderbilt House.* New York, 1925.

Warren, Garnet, and Cheney, Horace B. *The Romance of Design.* Garden City, N.Y.: Doubleday, Page, 1926.

Watson, Dudley Crafts. *Interior Decoration.* Chicago: American Library Association, 1932.

Weaver, Lawrence. "The Need for More Art in Industry." *American Magazine of Art* 19 (June 1928): 316–18.

"What's the Matter with the Modernists?" *American Magazine of Art* 17 (April 1926): 198–99.

"Where Are Our Moderns?" *Good Furniture and Decoration* 34 (March 1930): 9.

Wilcock, Arthur. "Use and Abuse of the Museum." *Good Furniture Magazine* 26 (February 1926): 81.

Wollin, Nils G. *Modern Swedish Decorative Art.* London: Architectural Press, 1931.

Sources Published after 1939

American Craft Museum. *For the Table Top.* New York, 1980.

Applegate, Judith. *Art Deco.* New York: Finch College Museum of Art, 1970.

Art in America 71 (March 1983): inside front cover. Illustration.

Arwas, Victor. *Art Deco.* London: Academy Editions, 1976.

Banham, Reyner. *Theory and Design in the First Machine Age.* Cambridge, Mass.: MIT Press, 1980. First published in 1960.

Baroni, Daniele, and D'Auria, Antonio. *Josef Hoffmann e la Wiener Werkstätte.* Milan: Electa, 1981.

Battersby, Martin. *The Decorative Thirties.* New York: Walker, 1971.

———. *The Decorative Twenties.* London: Studio Vista, 1969.

Bayer, Patricia, ed. *The Fine Art of the Furniture Maker.* Rochester, N.Y.: Memorial Art Gallery of the University of Rochester, 1981.

Bishop, Robert, and Coblentz, Patricia. *American Decorative Art: 360 Years of Creative Design.* New York: Harry N. Abrams, 1982.

Boardman, John. *Greek Art.* New York: Frederick A. Praeger, 1964.

Brunhammer, Yvonne. *Les Années "25": Collections du Musée des Arts Décoratifs.* Paris: Musée des Arts Décoratifs, 1966.

Bush, Donald J. *The Streamlined Decade.* New York: George Braziller, 1975.

Clark, Garth. *A Century of Ceramics in the United States, 1878–1978.* New York: E. P. Dutton in association with the Everson Museum of Art, 1979.

Clement, Arthur W. *Notes on American Ceramics: 1607–1943.* Brooklyn: Brooklyn Museum, Brooklyn Institute of Arts and Sciences, 1944.

Cox, Warren E. *The Book of Pottery and Porcelain.* 2 vols. New York: Crown Publishers, 1944.

De Syllas, Justin. "Streamform: Images of Speed and Greed from the 'Thirties.'" *Architectural Association Quarterly* 1 (April 1969): 32–41.

Detroit Institute of Arts. *Arts and Crafts in Detroit, 1906–1976: The Movement, The Society, The School.* Detroit, 1976.

Drexler, Arthur, and Daniel, Greta. *Introduction to Twentieth-Century Design from the Collection of The Museum of Modern Art.* New York: Museum of Modern Art, 1959.

Du Ry, Carel J. *The Art of Islam.* New York: Harry N. Abrams, 1970.

Ehresmann, Donald L. *Applied and Decorative Arts.* Littleton, Colo.: Libraries Unlimited, 1977.

Fagiolo dell'Arco, Maurizio. *Hoffmann: I Mobili Semplici, Vienna, 1900–1910.* Rome: Emporio Floreale, 1977.

Frégnac, Claude, et al. *French Cabinetmakers of the Eighteenth Century.* New York: French and European Publications, 1965.

Garner, Philippe. *Twentieth-Century Furniture.* New York: Van Nostrand Reinhold, 1980.

Gebhard, David. "The Moderne in the U.S., 1920–1941." *Architectural Association Quarterly* 2 (July 1970): 4–20.

Gowans, Alan. *Images of American Living: Four Centuries of Architecture and Furniture as Cultural Expression.* Philadelphia: Lippincott, 1964.

Greif, Martin. *Depression Modern: The Thirties Style in America.* New York: Universe Books, 1975.

Hanks, David A. *Innovative Furniture in America: From 1800 to the Present.* New York: Horizon Press, 1981.

Harris, Neil. "Museums, Merchandising, and Popular Taste: The Struggle for Influence." In *Material Culture and the Study of American Life,* ed. by Ian M. G. Quimby. New York: W. W. Norton, 1978. Pp. 140–74.

Heckscher Museum. *Art Deco and Its Origins.* Huntington, N.Y., 1974.

Herbert, Robert L. "Two Reliefs by Nola." *Yale University Art Gallery Bulletin* 34 (Winter 1974): 7–13.

Hillier, Bevis. *Art Deco.* Minneapolis, Minn.: Minneapolis Institute of Arts, 1971.

———. *Art Deco of the 20s and 30s.* London: Studio Vista, 1968.

Hughes, Graham. *Modern Silver throughout the World, 1880–1967.* New York: Crown Publishers, 1967.

Hunter, Penelope. "Art Deco and American Furniture." M.A. thesis, Institute of Fine Arts, New York University, 1971.

Hunter-Stiebel, Penelope. *The Metropolitan Museum of Art Bulletin* 37 (Winter 1979–80).

Indianapolis Museum of Art. *The Impact of Art Deco: 1925–1940.* Exhibition catalogue by Mary K. Grimes and Georgiann Gersell. Indianapolis, Ind., 1976.

Jenkins, Alan. *The Thirties.* New York: Stein and Day, 1976.

———. *The Twenties.* New York: Universe Books, 1974.

Kaufmann, Edgar, Jr. "Industrial Design in American Museums." *Magazine of Art* 42 (May 1949): 179–83.

Kinrose, Lord. "The Twenties." *The Architectural Review* 145 (May 1969): 317–24.

Klein, Dan. "The Chanin Building, New York." *The Connoisseur* 186 (July 1974): 162–69.

———. "The Chrysler Building." *The Connoisseur* 185 (April 1974): 294–301.

Krinsky, Carol Herselle. *Rockefeller Center.* New York: Oxford University Press, 1978.

Lackschewitz, Gertrud. *Interior Design and Decoration: A Bibliography.* New York: New York Public Library, 1961.

Lane, Barbara Miller. *Architecture and Politics in Germany, 1918–1945.* Cambridge, Mass.: Harvard University Press, 1968.

Lesieutre, Alain. *The Spirit and Splendour of Art Deco.* New York: Paddington Press, 1974.

Loewy, Raymond. *Industrial Design.* Woodstock, N.Y.: Overlook Press, 1979.

Loring, John. "American Deco." *The Connoisseur* 200 (January 1979): 48–53.

McClinton, Katharine Morrison. *Art Deco: A Guide for Collectors.* New York: Clarkson N. Potter, 1972.

Maenz, Paul. *Art Deco, Formen zwischen zwei Kriegen.* Cologne: Verlag M. DuMont Schauberg, 1974.

Meikle, Jeffrey L. *Twentieth Century Limited: Industrial Design in America, 1925–1939.* Philadelphia: Temple University Press, 1979.

Menten, Theodore, comp. *The Art Deco Style in Household Objects, Architecture, Sculpture, Graphics, Jewelry.* New York: Dover Publications, 1972.

Meyer, Christian. *Kolo Moser, Painter and Designer, 1868–1918.* Vienna: Galerie Metropol, 1983.

Miller, R. Craig, introd. "Frank Lloyd Wright at The Metropolitan Museum of Art." *The Metropolitan Museum of Art Bulletin* 40 (Fall 1982): 3.

Morningstar, Connie. *Flapper Furniture and Interiors of the 1920s.* Des Moines, Iowa: Wallace-Homestead, 1971.

Müller, Dorothee. *Klassiker des modernen Möbeldesign.* Munich: Keyser, 1980.

Musée des Arts Décoratifs, Paris. *Les Années "25": Art Déco/Bauhaus/Stijl/Esprit Nouveau.* Paris, 1966.

Ostrander, Gilman M. *American Civilization in the First Machine Age: 1890–
1940*. New York: Harper and Row,
1970.

Packard, Vance. *The Waste Makers*. New
York: David McKay, 1960.

Phillips, Lisa. *Shape and Environment: Fur-
niture by American Architects*. New
York: Whitney Museum of American
Art, 1982.

Plaut, James S. "Industrial Design in the
United States: Its Background and
Projects." *Perspectives USA* 9
(Autumn 1954): 118–36.

Plummer, Kathleen C. "The Streamlined
Moderne." *Art in America* 62 (January–February 1974): 46–54.

Polak, Ada. *Modern Glass*. London: Faber
and Faber, 1962.

Prather-Moses, Alice Irma, comp. "The
International Dictionary of Women
Workers in the Decorative Arts: A
Survey of the Twentieth Century from
1900 to 1975." Unpublished manu-
script. Forthcoming volume to sup-
plement Prather-Moses, Alice Irma,
comp. *The International Dictionary of
Women Workers in the Decorative
Arts*. Metuchen, N.J.: Scarecrow
Press, 1981.

Pulos, Arthur J. *American Design Ethic: A
History of Industrial Design to 1940*.
Cambridge, Mass.: MIT Press, 1983.

Renwick Gallery. *The Designs of Raymond
Loewy*. Washington, D.C.: Smithsonian Institution Press, 1975.

Robinson, Cervin, and Bletter, Rosemarie
Haag. *Skyscraper Style: Art Deco
New York*. New York: Oxford Univer-
sity Press, 1975.

Robsjohn-Gibbings, T. H. *Homes of the
Brave*. New York: Alfred A. Knopf,
1954.

Rosenthal, Rudolph, and Ratzka, Helena L.
The Story of Modern Applied Art.
New York: Harper and Brothers,
1948.

Rothmans of Pall Mall Canada Limited.
*Deco, 1925–1935, Presented by
Rothmans*. 1975.

Sembach, Klaus-Jürgen. *Into the Thirties—
Style and Design 1927–1934*. London: Thames and Hudson, 1972.

Sheon, Aaron. "Lucien Rollin, Architecte-
Décorateur of the 1930s: French
Modern Furniture Design vs. German
Functionalism." *Arts Magazine* 56
(May 1982): 104–18.

Soule, George. *Prosperity Decade: From
War to Depression, 1917–1929*. New
York: Rinehart, 1947.

Stiles, Helen E. *Pottery in the United States*.
New York: E. P. Dutton, 1941.

Tarbell, Roberta K. *Hugo Robus, 1885–
1964*. Washington, D.C.: Smithsonian Institution Press for the National
Collection of Fine Arts, 1980.

Tunnard, Christopher, and Reed, Henry
Hope. *American Skyline: The Growth
and Form of Our Cities and Towns*.
Boston: Houghton-Mifflin, 1955.

Venturi, Robert. *Complexity and Contradic-
tion in Architecture*. New York:
Museum of Modern Art, 1977.
Rev. ed.

Veronesi, Giulia. *Style and Design, 1909–
1929*. New York: George Braziller,
1968.

Wilk, Christopher. *Marcel Breuer: Furniture
and Interiors*. New York: Museum of
Modern Art, 1981.

———. *Thonet: 150 Years of Furniture*.
Woodbury, N.Y.: Barrron's Educational Series, 1980.

Zorach, William. *Art Is My Life*. Cleveland:
World, 1967.

Photographs of objects reproduced in the
catalogue have been provided in many
cases by custodians of the works. The following list applies to photographs for
which additional acknowledgment is due.

Armen Photographers, cat. 21; E. Irving
Blomstrann, cats. 9, 10, 13, 14, 15, 38, 42,
44, 56, 67, 69, 80, 81; Richard P. Good-
body, cat. 23; Scott Hyde, fig. 6, cat. 27;
Dennis McWaters, cat. 2; Geri T. Mancini,
cats. 47, 60, 70, 73; Mark Meachem, cat
58, courtesy Washburn Gallery, New York
City; Northlight Studio, cats. 1, 46, 54;
Michael J. Peters, cats. 24, 25, 37, 64;
David Stansbury, cat. 29; Duane Suter,
cat. 40; Joseph Szaszfai, cats. 18, 47, 59,
60, 70, 74; Charles Uht, cats. 3, 4, 5, 7, 10,
11, 16, 20, 22, 23, 26, 27, 32, 33, 34, 35,
36, 41, 43, 48, 50, 51, 52, 55, 57, 61, 63,
71, 76, 78.

Boldface numerals refer to catalogue numbers and indicate the principal source of information on designers and manufacturers represented in the exhibition. Page numbers are in light type; footnotes are designated by the letter n.

At Home In Manhattan is set in a film version of Futura, a typeface conceived by Ferdinand Kramer in 1925. Kramer was a student of Paul Renner, an architect, painter and book designer, who re-worked the drawings and had them cast into type at the Bauer Type Foundry, Frankfurt, in 1928. The "machine made" appearance of the letters relates to decorative arts of the period.

The text was composed by Custom Typographic Service, Inc., Hamden, Connecticut, and printed by Rembrandt Press, Milford, Connecticut, on Warren's Lustro Offset Enamel Dull, cream.

The catatogue was designed by Karen Salsgiver. Production was supervised by Yale University Printing Service.

The cover is based on the design of a rug by Ruth Reeves called "Electric"